W9-CAJ-321

Portugal

Portugal

BY ETTAGALE BLAUER
AND JASON LAURÉ

Enchantment of the World
Second Series

Children's Press®
A Division of Scholastic Inc.
NEW YORK TORONTO LONDON AUCKLAND SYDNEY
MEXICO CITY NEW DELHI HONG KONG
DANBURY, CONNECTICUT

Frontispiece: Portuguese girl in local costume

Consultant: Dr. Amy J. Johnson, Ph.D., Assistant Professor of History, Berry College, Mount Berry, Georgia

Please note: All statistics are as up-to-date as possible at the time of publication.

Book production by Herman Adler Design

Library of Congress Cataloging-in-Publication Data

Blauer, Ettagale
Portugal / by Ettagale Blauer and Jason Lauré
p. cm. — (Enchantment of the world. Second series)
Includes bibliographical references and index.
ISBN 0-516-21109-9
1. Portugal—Juvenile literature. [1. Portugal.] I. Lauré, Jason. II. Title. III. Series.
DP517 .B53 2002
946.9—dc21 2001047723

1 2 3 4 5 6 7 8 9 10 R 11 10 09 08 07 06 05 04 03 02

Acknowledgments

Our special thanks go to Nelson de Carvalho, instructor of Portuguese language and culture at Escola do Encino Basico de Pelheiras in Lisbon, for his insights on the integration of Angolans into Portugal; to Luis Peres for sharing his knowledge of the culture and of children's games; to the staff at the English-language school in Lisbon; to the guides at the Camões Institute and the Gulbenkian Museum; to Luis de Carvalho for showing us the neighborhood life of Lumiar; to Kimberly da Costa Holton for her knowledge of *fado*; to Michael Teague for the history of Portugal; and to the many others who were so helpful to us over the years.

Cover photo:
A peaceful harbor in the Algarve

Contents

CHAPTER

ONE Exploring the World 8

TWO A Country at the End of the World 14

THREE A Look at Nature 30

FOUR Many Threads Come Together 40

FIVE Ruling Portugal 68

SIX Earning a Living 74

SEVEN The Changing Face of Portugal 92

EIGHT A Nation of Catholics 100

NINE Leisure Time the Portuguese Way 106

TEN A Unique Way of Life 118

National Palace

Timeline **128**

Fast Facts **130**

To Find Out More **134**

Index **136**

Children in traditional dress

Exploring the World

Portugal is proof that a small nation can shape the history of the world. When Portuguese sailors set off into the Atlantic Ocean more than 500 years ago, they were following the dreams of their ruler—Prince Henry the Navigator. Their voyages changed the future in ways that we are still dealing with today. What the Portuguese did 500 years ago set the stage for colonization, and for slavery. Who would imagine that journeys taken in small boats in the distant past could still have an impact on life in the United States five centuries later?

Opposite: **Prince Henry was instrumental in early Portuguese exploration and discovery.**

Portugal's sailors were the "astronauts" of their day. Although their voyages were extremely dangerous, they were based on the best scientific knowledge of the time. The Portuguese used an instrument called the astrolabe to help them

The astrolabe helped sailors navigate at sea.

Caravels carried explorers on their journeys around the world.

know their position at sea and to help guide them on their journeys. They sailed in caravels, beautiful wooden ships with large sails, and wherever they went, they claimed land for Portugal. Thus they created a series of colonies around the world.

The Portuguese came to call this time the "Age of the Discoveries." At that time, Europeans knew very little about the lands that lay off their shores. Some of these lands were just hundreds of miles away while others were many thousands of miles in the distance.

As they roamed the world's oceans, the Portuguese sailors left traces of their journeys. They left markers along the shore

Marker left in 1486 by Portuguese explorer Diogo Cão at Cape Cross in Namibia.

Fort Jesus at Mombasa built by Portuguese explorers in 1593.

of Africa to prove that they had made their groundbreaking trips. One still stands at Cape Cross in Namibia where Diogo Cão landed in 1485. Statues marking their journeys may be found in many countries including one in Mossel Bay, South Africa, which portrays Bartolomeu Dias, one of Portugal's best-known explorers. After the first explorers touched the African shore, others followed, building forts to protect themselves, including the fort at Mombasa, in Kenya, on the Indian Ocean.

Soon, Portuguese settlers began to arrive in these areas. They found the environments very difficult to live in. Many of the people living in these lands were hostile to the new-comers. The Portuguese wanted to profit from their travels by finding goods they could ship home or use in trade. They began to take humans as slaves.

Geopolitical map of Portugal

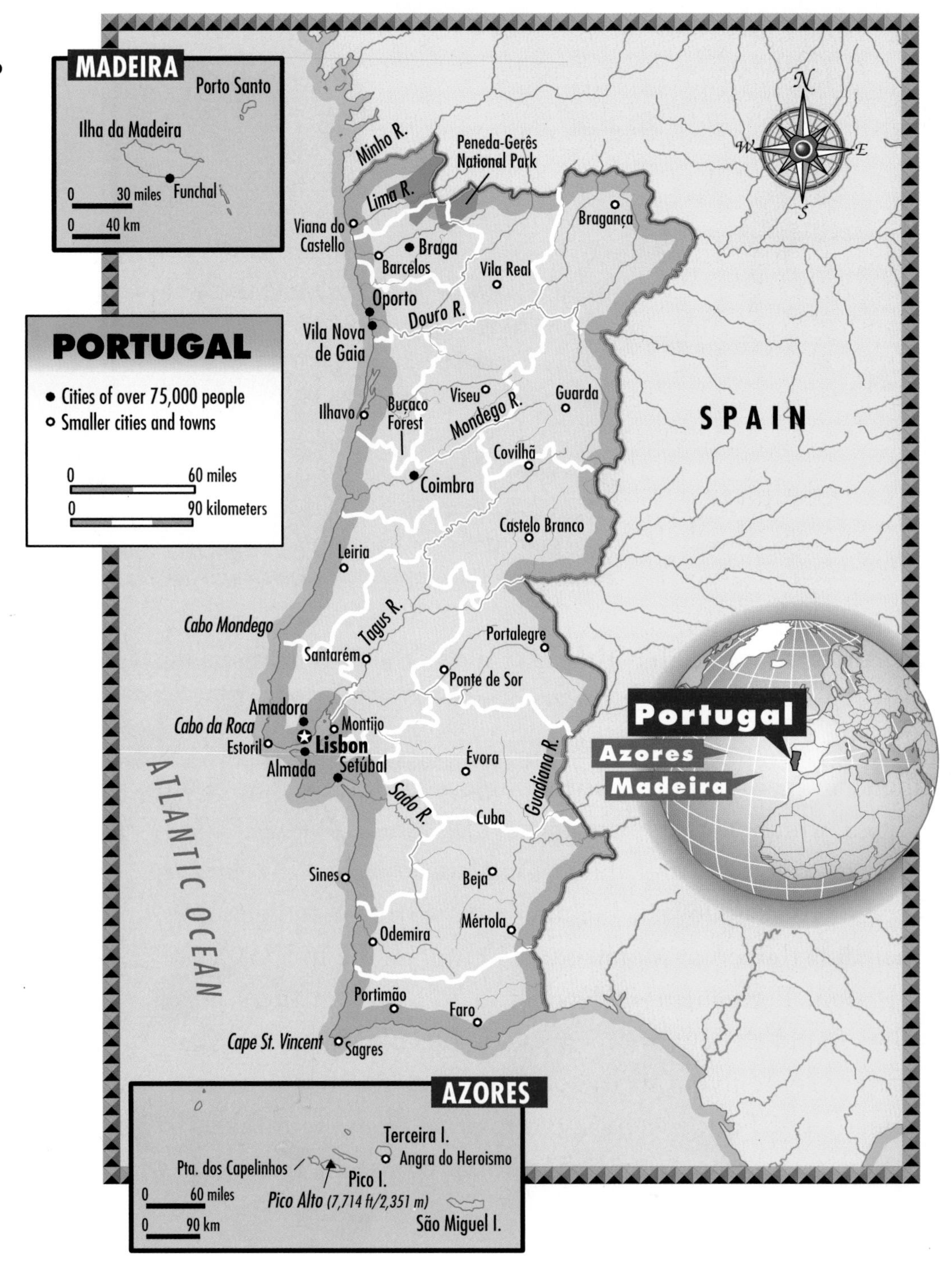

We'll look into these journeys and the way they changed the world. Although these trips took place so long ago, they shaped the nation of Portugal and the Portuguese people. They spread the Portuguese language to distant lands where it is spoken by 200 million people. Today, it is the eighth most-spoken language in the world. For the Europeans, the journeys answered questions about parts of the world that were previously unknown to them. At the same time, they totally changed the course of the development of much of the continent of Africa and its peoples. Millions of Africans were shipped out as slaves, never to see their homes and their homelands again. No one knows how vast regions of Africa would have developed if the Europeans, including the Portuguese, had not explored, settled, and claimed these territories.

Today, the Portuguese people are still trying to understand their own history and their role as a colonial power. Their colonial empire ended when they gave up control of Macao on China's coast, their last colony. Today, Portugal's history as a great seafaring nation and as a country of explorers is something Portuguese children read about in history books. The Portuguese make trips to Cabo da Roca, the westernmost point in continental Europe, to look out over the sea and remember a time when Portugal was a great nation. They once looked at the sea and faraway lands as a solution to their problems. Today, they are trying to work out their problems while becoming more integrated into the rest of Europe, through the European Union.

A Country at the End of the World

PORTUGAL IS LOCATED AT THE WESTERNMOST POINT OF CONtinental Europe. It was described by the famous Portuguese poet Luis de Camões as the place "where land ends and sea begins." It clings to the edge of the Iberian peninsula—a piece of land that juts out into the Atlantic Ocean. Portugal occupies just one-sixth of the peninsula while Spain occupies the remainder. Its physical location has kept Portugal separate from the rest of Europe. It helped to turn Portugal into a nation that looked out at the sea and set its sights on distant lands. The country's unusual geography is one of the most important facts in understanding the history of Portugal.

Opposite: **Land meeting the sea on the Algarve Coast.**

The country covers a total of 35,550 square miles (92,080 square kilometers) including the islands of the Azores which measure 879 square miles (2,278 sq km), and Madeira, which measures 304 square miles (788 sq km). The Atlantic Ocean forms Portugal's borders to the west and south while Spain borders Portugal to the east and north. The coastline of mainland Portugal stretches for 1,114 miles (1,793 km). The land borders shared with Spain measure 754 miles (1,214 km). The country is slightly smaller than the state of Indiana. The shape is roughly rectangular with the length running north and south and the width running east and west.

Although small in size, Portugal's landscape and topography vary tremendously from north to south. These differences have shaped the lives its people live, the way they earn their

Portugal's Geographic Features

Area: 35,550 square miles (92,080 sq km)

Highest Elevation: Estrela, in Serra da Estrela, 6,539 feet (1,993 m)

Lowest Elevation: Sea level along the Atlantic Ocean

Longest River: Tagus (Tejo) 626 miles (1,000 km), including Spain

Largest Reservoir: Rocha da Gale Reservoir on the Guadiana

Greatest Annual Precipitation: 110 inches (279 cm) in Serra da Estrela

Length of Coastline: 1,114 miles (1,793 km)

Most Recent Volcanic Activity: Terceira, Azores, on January 8, 1999

Greatest Distance: 350 miles (563 km), north to south; 140 miles (201 km), east to west

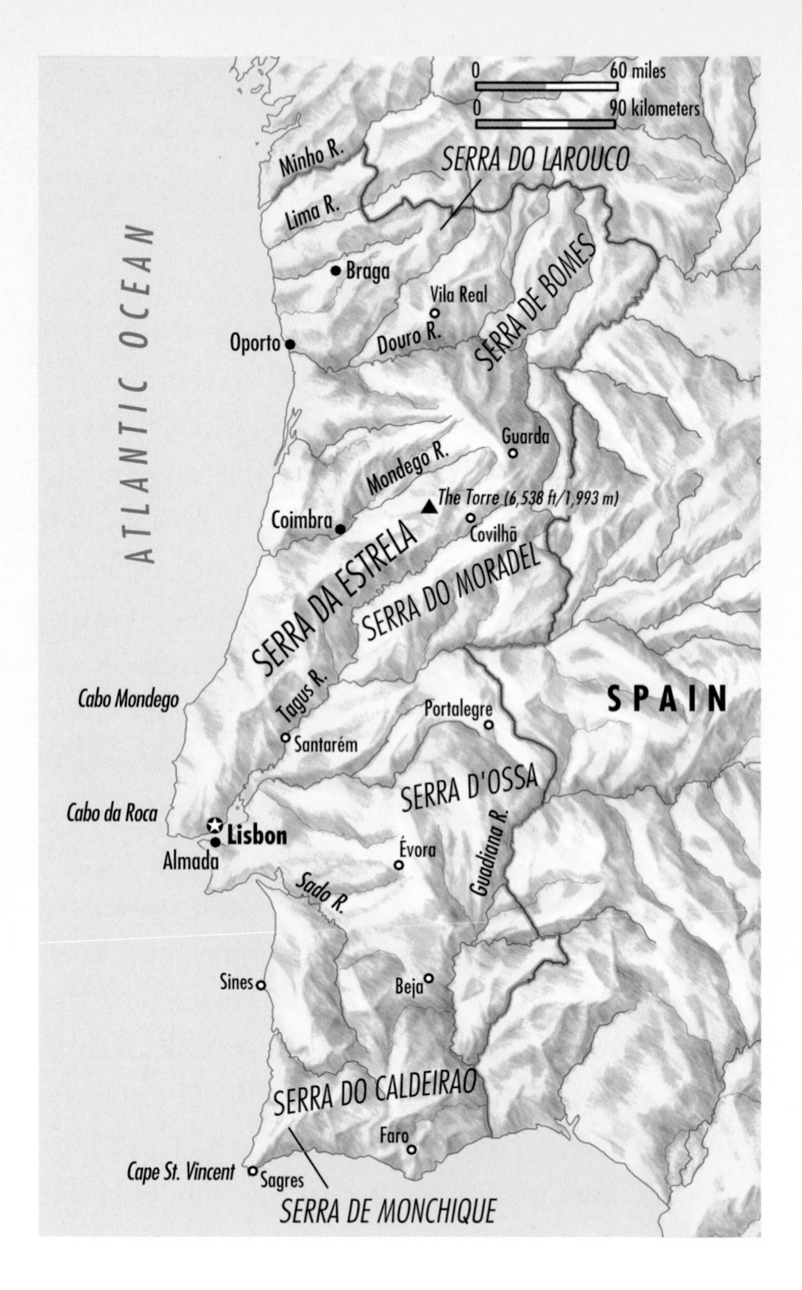

living, and how they view neighboring Spain. Spain not only forms two of Portugal's borders, it actually wraps around the nation, blocking it off from physical contact with any other country.

Six Regions

The country has six regions that reflect the different geographical features separating them. Starting in the north, these six are the Minho and Trás-os-Monte; Beira, Estremadura, Alentejo, and Algarve in the south. Although these old provinces have now been divided into smaller districts for governing, the names are still used to refer to the regions just as people in the United States speak about the Northwest, the East, the South, and the Midwest.

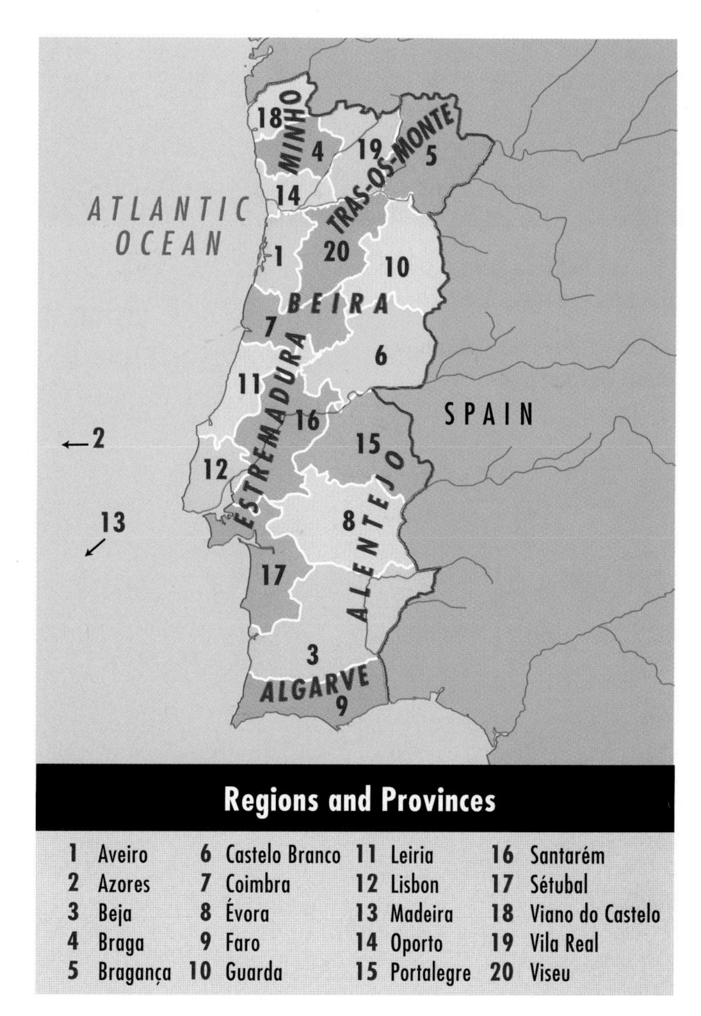

The northernmost part of the country is very hilly. Most of the land here lies above 1,300 feet (396 meters) and is broken up into plateaus with great valleys between them. Near the ocean, mountains rise as high as 3,000 feet (914 m) just 30 miles (48 km) from the shore. In the extreme northwest, at the border with Spain, the Serra do Larouco rises 5,003 feet (1,525 m). The landscape is dramatically cut by rivers that flow along deep gorges. Another mountain range marks the province of Trás-os-Monte e Alto Douro. The highest point on mainland Portugal is Torre, in the Serra da Estrela mountain range,

at 6,539 feet (1,993 m). Here the rivers flow through canyons 1,600 feet (488 m) deep. Many of Portugal's small farms and vineyards are found here, although the land is very rocky and difficult to farm. The highest peak of all is in the Azores, the island group that forms one of Portugal's maritime provinces. The peak is Pico Alto, which stands 7,714 feet (2,351 m) high.

Above: **Hillside homes dot the mountainous landscape.**

Below: **Rivers flow through deep gorges in the Serra do Larouco.**

The Douro River winds its way through Oporto.

Portugal's principal rivers, the Douro in the north and the Tagus, (*Tejo*), in the south, separate the country into three regions. The north is the smallest region, occupying about one-fifth of the land, while the rest of the land is divided almost equally into the central and southern regions.

Much of the central region is a high plain. The division between this region and the north is formed by the Serra da Estrela, a barrier made of granite and schist that stands like a great wall. The central plains of the country are heavily farmed with olive trees, wheat, tomatoes, and trees with bark used to make cork.

The South

Most of the southern part of Portugal is called the *Alentejo*, a word that means "beyond the Tagus." This name describes the land that lies south of the Tagus River. It is a major farming area. The farms are larger and the gently rolling land is better suited to farming. The most southern region of Portugal is called the Algarve. This area is different in feeling from the

Fine white sand and tall cliffs along an Algarve beach

rest of Portugal, partly because the region is cut off by mountains and by the influence of the Moors, the people of North Africa who conquered this area in the eighth century. Their influence can be seen in the architecture and culture. The climate here is quite warm and there are many days of sunshine each year. The cliffs that rise up along the southernmost part of the Algarve block winds and shelter the sandy beaches below. The Serra do Monchique mountains form another barrier in the south, creating an even greater separation between the Alentejo and the Algarve.

The Islands

The islands of Madeira and the Azores are considered part of Portugal. The Azores, a group of nine islands, lie 800 miles (1,300 km) west of Portugal in the Atlantic Ocean. This distant outpost is home to about 240,000 people. When the islands were discovered in 1427, they were uninhabited. They were settled by the Portuguese.

Azores

Each of the nine islands has a distinct look and culture and the Azores, as a group, are a small world of natural beauty. The islands are actually the remains of volcanoes that are still active. They have rugged landscapes and are known for the contrast between the black basalt thrown up by the volcanoes and the brilliant blue and green seawater that surrounds them. Because they lie in the path of the Gulf Stream, the climate on the Azores is usually mild and humid. In the late 1950s, an entirely

The Azores are known for their temperate climate and rugged landscape.

new piece of land was created from lava spewing out of a volcano called Capelinhos. The highest point in the Azores is the Pico volcano rising 1,461 miles (2,351 m) on Pico Island. The city of Angra do Heroísmo on the island of Terceira was named a World Heritage Site in 1983 because of its seventeenth- and eighteenth-century buildings including churches and palaces.

Madeira

The archipelago of Madeira is also in the Atlantic Ocean, west of the African country of Morocco. These islands were found by accident in 1419, when Portuguese explorers were blown off course by storms. The main island was named *Ilha da Madeira*, which means "the island of wood" because of its great forests. Uninhabited when they were discovered, the Madeira islands are now home to 280,000 people. The capital and main city of Funchal was named for the wild fennel that grows nearby. Some visitors reach Madeira on cruise ships that stop there for one or two days.

Blessed with Rivers

Portugal is a land watered with ten major rivers. The Tagus, the longest river in Portugal, is known as the *Rio Tejo* in Portuguese. It begins its journey in Spain and flows westward across Portugal, nearly at the midpoint of the country. It continues its way to Lisbon where it empties into the Atlantic Ocean. It travels for about 150 miles (241 km) across Portugal. The Tagus carves its way around Lisbon and creates a beautiful setting for the city. Many of the city's important monuments are found along the river's shores with a commanding view of the Tagus.

In Lisbon, Santa Engracia's dome can be seen from the Tagus River.

Bridges Over the Tagus

Two major bridges span the Tagus at Lisbon. The 25th of April Bridge (*Ponte 25 de Abril*) was built in 1966. It was originally called the Salazar Bridge. After the revolution of April 25, 1974, its name was changed. The bridge carries many workers in cars and trains to the suburbs across the river. When it was built, it was the longest suspension bridge in Europe. Now, Lisbon has the Vasco da Gama Bridge (pictured), a 10-mile (16-km) -long bridge that was built for Expo '98, the world's fair. It also marked the 500th anniversary of Vasco da Gama's successful voyage to the east. The bridge was designed to remind visitors of the sailing ships used in the days of the explorers. Much of the bridge is built close to the water, giving travelers a spectacular view as they make their way across the Tagus, which is very wide at this point.

The Douro River takes its name from Portuguese words that mean "of gold" because the river seems to glow like a golden chain of gold as it snakes its way through the valley.

A Look at Portugal's Cities

Oporto (pictured), located at the mouth of the Douro River, is Portugal's second-largest city with a population of about 310,000. Oporto's harbor provides shipping

and transportation in the northern region of Portugal. Port wine, which gets its name from Oporto, has been a major moneymaker in that region for centuries. Oporto mixes modern architecture and business with a history that goes back to the Roman Empire. A major landmark in the city's center is the cathedral, built during the twelfth century. The Arrábida Bridge spanning the Douro was the longest concrete-arch bridge in Europe before the Vasco da Gama Bridge was built.

Coimbra, with a population of about 148,000, lies in west-central Portugal on the Mondego River. The city was settled by Romans and originally called Aeminium. Today, Coimbra is an agricultural distribution center, as well as a manufacturing center for ceramic, paper and wood pulp, textiles, leather goods, and food processing. The University of Coimbra is Portugal's oldest university. Originally located in Lisbon, the university moved to Coimbra in 1537. In the town center, the Old Cathedral, built in the 1100s, rises high above the surrounding buildings.

The city of Sintra, with a population of 20,574, is a major tourist destination located 12 miles (20 km) west of Lisbon. The region was controlled by Moors from A.D. 711 to 1147 and reminders of Moorish art and architecture are found throughout Sintra. Tourists flock to the Sintra Mountains and historic sites, such as the Palácio da Pena. The Castelo dos Mouros in Sintra is more than 1,300 years old.

Funchal, the capital of Madeira, is a seaside paradise. Home to about 120,000 Portuguese, the city swells with tourists during spring and summer. Visitors enjoy the São Francisco Cellars Wine Museum and the Museum of Sacred Art. The Wine Museum displays the tools of the ancient art of wine making, including a seventeenth-century wine press, historical labels, and a working barrel-making operation. The Museum of Sacred Art is housed in the Old Episcopal Court on Bishop's Road. The art works include statuary, sculpture, painting, and religious jewelry collected from throughout Portugal.

Vineyards of the Duoro River Valley

It runs for about 130 miles (210 km) across Portugal through the beautiful countryside covered by carefully tended vineyards and empties into the Atlantic Ocean at Oporto.

The third major river to make its way through Portugal is the Guadiana, which forms part of the border with Spain. In some places, the Guadiana widens until it seems more like a lake than a river. It continues to run southward, through part of the Alentejo until it reaches the Algarve. Here, it again forms the border between Portugal and Spain until it empties into the Gulf of Cadiz. The Guadiana runs for about 115 miles (185 km) within Portugal. Many other small rivers crisscross Portugal.

Climate

Rainfall throughout the country usually occurs from October through March. This makes Portugal a good choice for tourists who enjoy sunny days for their sightseeing. Equally important, this predictable rainfall gives farmers a tremendous advantage. They can plant their crops and know just when they will get rain.

Even though Portugal does not border on the great Mediterranean Sea, it has what is often called a "Mediterranean climate." This means that the weather is pleasantly warm and comfortable for most of the year in much of the country. In the northwest, summers are short but the long winters are mild. Most of the rain falls in the winter. The northeast is quite different with its short, hot summers. In the south, rain falls mainly in early spring and autumn. The weather can be very warm, sometimes hot, depending on the worldwide climate. One recent spring saw the temperature rise to nearly 100° Fahrenheit (37.7° Celsius) in Lisbon. In the mountains of the Trás-os-Monte, in the northeast, winters can be extremely cold. In the Algarve, which faces south, winter is usually very pleasant and mild, thanks in part to the warming breezes. However, the Algarve pays a price for its warm winters with extremely hot and dry summers.

End of the World

The dramatic name *fin do mundo*, or "end of the world," is often given to a point of land called Cabo da Roca. This is the westernmost point of land in continental Europe. A working lighthouse

The Earthquake of 1755

On November 1, 1755, Portugal's churches were full of people marking All Saints' Day. Suddenly, a massive earthquake hit Lisbon. At least 5,000 people were

killed immediately, and many more died in fires and of disease and famine in the following weeks. A huge tidal wave swept over the city, taking many of the survivors to their death. As many as 40,000 people may have been killed, an enormous number considering the population at that time was estimated at 275,000. Lisbon was one of the largest cities in Europe.

Sebastião José de Carvalho e Melo, also known as the Marquês de Pombal (right), was the powerful ruler of Portugal under King José I. Pombal was very interested in forcing ideas on Portugal that he had learned while serving as ambassador to Great Britain and Austria. The disastrous earthquake gave Pombal exactly the situation he needed. He was a master at organizing everything. After taking care of the injured and setting up temporary services for food and shelter, he turned to the idea of building an entirely new city of Lisbon.

Architect Eugenio dos Santos and engineer Manuel da Maia came up with a plan for this new city. After the rubble was cleared away, they divided the land into long, grand avenues. Dramatic views were highlighted by important squares that gave the city its commercial centers. Their work can still be seen in Lisbon. It served the city well at the time and provides Lisbon today with a traffic plan that helps to move cars, buses, and trucks swiftly through the heart of the city.

stands up on the cliffs that look out over the Atlantic Ocean. To the west, the ocean stretches out to the horizon. This isolated point makes it possible to get a sense of how the early explorers must have felt. It gives one a feeling of truly being at the end of the world that was known to Europeans. For the sailors, there was no way of knowing when they would see their homeland again. Visitors to Cabo da Roca can have their names written on a certificate that shows they were at this westernmost point.

Cabo da Roca, the westernmost point of land in continental Europe, feels like being at "the end of the world."

Unusual Geography

Portugal's location at the entrance to the Mediterranean Sea has been important to its history. Invasions from both sea and land were made possible by the short distance between Portugal and the countries that ring the sea, especially those of North Africa. Portugal was said to "look to Africa" and not to Europe for its connections with the world. It felt cut off from the rest of Europe because of its position in the extreme west of the continent. Africa, on the other hand, was just a short trip across the ocean and the Portuguese were very good at making that sea journey.

THREE

A Look at Nature

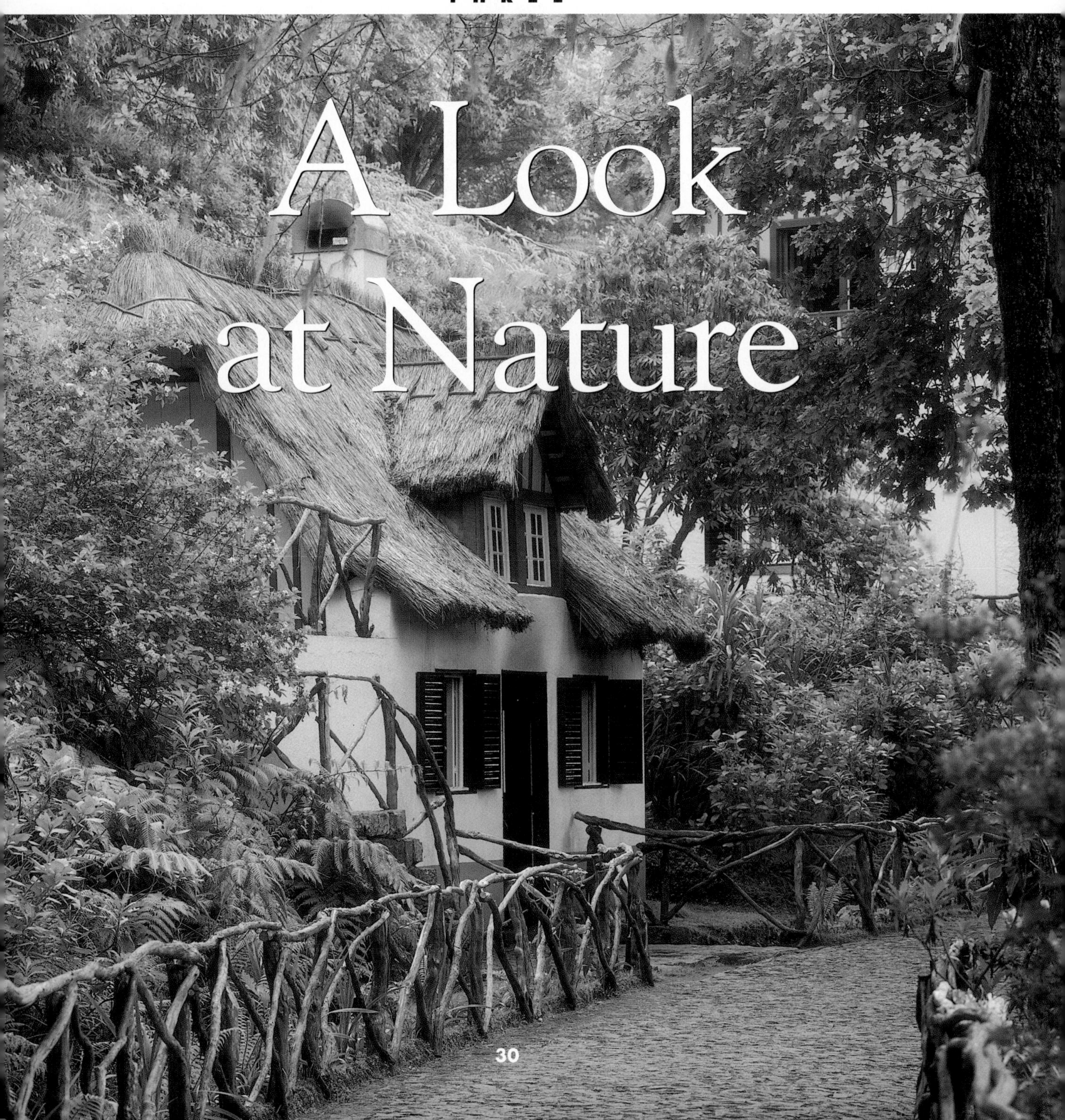

THE PORTUGUESE PEOPLE LOVE FLOWERING PLANTS AND grow colorful flowers such as hydrangea and bougainvillea around their homes and apartments. Pots of flowering plants are placed to catch the sun on almost every little balcony or windowsill. The hilly streets of Lisbon are dotted with flowers. Along the main boulevards, formal gardens include grand old trees and hedges clipped into geometric patterns. At major intersections, where traffic circles allow as many as eight roads to come together, there is usually a statue surrounded by greenery, and often flower beds too.

Above left: **Bougainvillea wind around a lamppost.**

Above right: **The Zoological Gardens in Lisbon display the clipped hedges of a formal garden.**

Opposite: **Flowers surround a home in Madeira.**

Most Portuguese still earn their living as farmers even though the land in Portugal is very difficult to work. The soil is poor and the climate, while delightful for visitors, can be devastating to a farmer who depends on the weather. Portuguese farmers struggle to produce their crops of maize (a type of corn), wheat, and potatoes.

The Forests of Portugal

Portugal's best crop and certainly its most native are the trees that grow in its forests. Just a few centuries ago, nearly all of Portugal was covered with great oak forests. Today, only about one-third of the country is forested. In areas where forest cover has been lost, efforts are underway to replace this important natural resource. The first replanting took place in the center of Portugal, north of the Tagus River. Forested areas help to maintain a moderate climate. When large forests are lost, the land is unable to hold onto rainfall and the topsoil may be washed away. This leaves behind dry, baked earth.

Forested area of the Algarve

In addition to the traditional oak trees that make up most of the forests, Portugal imported the distinctive eucalyptus tree from Australia about 150 years ago. Eucalyptus leaves have a very strong scent. Grown on about 15 percent of the forested land, eucalyptus has many uses. Eucalyptus oil is used in medicines for coughs and colds. The pulp from the trees is used to make paper for the printing industry.

An unusual variety of oak tree called the cork oak grows in the Alentejo. Cork trees have a distinctive shape. Instead of growing straight up like pine trees, these trees tend to spread out. Their trunks are knotty-looking. The trees are harvested in a unique way to produce cork. Portugal supplies about half of all the cork used in the world. Cork is popular because it is extremely light in weight yet it has the ability to keep wine and champagne fresh in the bottle. It also makes excellent soundproofing material, and it is even used inside spacecraft where weight is a particular concern.

Cork trees are a common sight in the Alentejo.

Put Some Cork In It

Although cork appears to be spongy, it does not easily absorb water so it is an extremely useful substance. In addition to plugging champagne and wine bottles, cork is used for making floor and wall coverings. Cork gaskets are an essential part of car and airplane engines. Portuguese cork gaskets are even found in the U.S. space shuttle. Cork forms the surface of bulletin boards, the soles of shoes, and the centers of baseballs.

Gardens, Plants, and Flowers

In the heart of Lisbon, the capital city, the *Jardim Botanico* (Botanical Garden) brings together exotic plants from Portugal's former colonies and features palm trees that are more than 100 years old. The garden was created in 1873 and includes banana trees, bamboo, and water lilies. It displays some of the 2,700 species of plants found in Portugal. Nearly all of these were brought to Portugal. Only about ninety species are native to Portugal.

A similar garden, known as the Bucaco Forest, is found in the far-northern region called Beira. There, Carmelite monks began to cultivate species of trees that Portuguese sailors brought back from distant lands. Today, 700 varieties of trees are found here, including Himalayan pines, Japanese camphor trees, and Lebanese cedars.

In the Algarve, almond trees were planted long, long ago. When the almond tree blooms, its snowy white or pink blossoms are a magical sight. A legend claims that the almond trees were introduced to Portugal by a Moorish prince from North Africa to remind his wife of their homeland because these blossoms look like the snow on the Atlas Mountains. After the blossoms fall, the almonds grow and are harvested in the summer.

Snow-white blossoms cover almond trees before the almonds grow.

The carob tree is seen throughout the south too and is sometimes called the "tree of life" because its beans can be eaten and also used to make oil. An unusual tree, the loquat, produces small fruits like plums.

In the wine district around Oporto, the steep hillsides are covered with vineyards, set on terraces. Every inch of land is cultivated and carefully maintained.

The province of Minho, just north of Oporto, is sometimes called the *Costa Verde*, which means "Green Coast." The green comes from the vineyards and from the many plants cultivated here. The vineyards here are so tiny, often just 1 or 2 acres (0.4 or 0.8 hectares) that the farmers have created a two-tier system of cultivation. They train the grapevines upward, along the trees and hedges, even along the walls of their homes. They also plant crops such as potatoes and onions.

A Year of Fruits and Flowers

The almond blossoms of January and February are followed by orange blossoms and acacias in March. In April, wildflowers bloom. May and June bring out the brilliant jacaranda flowering trees. In July, cherries, strawberries, and melons brighten Portugal's markets. August and September bring grapes, figs, and almond crops, while November is the month to gather chestnuts. In December, the Algarve orange-picking season begins, and the year ends as sweetly as it began.

National Symbol

Portugal's national symbol, the cockerel, or rooster, began as an emblem of its religious belief. The Cockerel of Suffering is part of the imagery of the Roman Catholic Church and figures prominently in the Festival of Senhor Santo Cristo that takes place in the Azores. The cockerel is a popular symbol that appears on handicrafts of all kinds including the small figurines sold everywhere. It is also used on dinnerware and as a decoration on many household objects.

Loss of Habitat

In 2001, the Portuguese government began a project that will have a tremendous impact on the natural environment of the Alentejo. A dam, planned to be built on the Guadiana River, will flood a 40-square-mile (104-sq-km) area. The Alqueva Dam will be the largest in Europe, creating an artificial lake with the greatest surface area. It has been in the planning for thirty years. Although people supporting the construction of the dam say it will benefit farmers, many believe it is really intended to increase tourism in the area. Tourists would come for the water sports that are usually created around a dam.

The golden eagle's habitat will be eliminated by the Alqueva Dam's construction.

Half the enormous cost of the project, estimated at $407 million, came from the European Union. The dam is supposed to generate hydroelectric power and also to create 20,000 jobs but many dispute these figures. Others believe the benefits of the dam will not make up for the environmental destruction. More than 1 million trees will be cut down to make way for the dam. This will eliminate the natural habitats of many birds and animals including the golden eagle and the Iberian lynx.

The Iberian Lynx

The lynx is a small, spotted wildcat with pointed ears, a beautiful coat, and whiskers around its chin. A small number of lynx still survive in isolated parts of Portugal. Some are found in the mountains of the Algarve and others live close to the border with Spain. The species is near extinction because not more than a few hundred Iberian lynx are still known to be alive today. Their numbers declined because they were hunted by farmers, and because their natural food—wild rabbits—died out.

Lusitano Horse

The Lusitano species of horse developed thousands of years ago on the Iberian Peninsula, which includes modern Portugal and Spain. The horses were well known in the region and were even written about by Homer in the *Iliad* around 700 B.C. The Lusitano horse is very sturdy, with a strong neck and shoulders. Its shorter build and great strength makes it useful in bullfights. The horses stand up bravely to the charges of the powerful bull.

Portuguese Water Dogs

No one really knows how the *caes de agua* (Portuguese water dog) originally came to Portugal. Some say it arrived with the Berbers of North Africa in the 700s. Others think it may have come to the region with the Visigoths, as early as A.D. 400. Regardless of how it arrived, the Portuguese water dog has become a breed of legend. In 1927, a Portuguese water dog was reported to have saved a sailor from drowning. Several other species including French poodles, Irish water spaniels, Kerry blue terriers, and Labrador retrievers evolved from the Portuguese water dog.

They are also quick to respond to the rider's commands. The Lusitano horse is also seen at Portuguese riding and jumping events including the Fair at Golega.

The Lusitano horse was first bred as long ago as 700 B.C.

Many Threads Come Together

Portugal's earliest history was a continual struggle against invaders from other lands. Its location put the area in the path of aggressive outsiders who first conquered the local people and then settled among them. Each wave of conquest left its mark on the language, the architecture, the knowledge, and even on the farming methods of the people.

Opposite: **Roman ruins in Conimbriga are a reminder of ancient conquerers of Portugal.**

The area we now call Portugal has been inhabited for at least 10,000 years. The region's many rivers, especially the Tagus River, created a pleasant environment in which people could live. These people hunted and fished for food. We know what they ate because of the bones and shells of the animals and shellfish they left behind. People who live by hunting and fishing often move around as they search for food.

About 5,000 years ago, people began to farm the land. Farmers are settled people who live and grow crops on a certain piece of land.

Over the next 2,000 years, through the Stone Age, the Bronze Age, and the Iron Age, various peoples lived in settled communities on the Iberian Peninsula. They left behind tools and other objects that tell us of their presence, and of how they lived.

Waves of migrants arrived over the next thousand years, including the Phoenicians who arrived on the west coast. After them came the Celts, who traveled overland from Europe. These people built forts in northern Portugal.

Roman Iberia, 1st & 2nd Centuries

The Romans conquered the entire peninsula in the third century B.C. Although the local people, called Lusitanians, fiercely resisted the Romans, they were unable to stop Rome's powerful and determined armies. At its height, the Roman Empire stretched over a vast territory around the Mediterranean Sea.

The Romans made the Lusitanians part of their empire by ruling through local administration. The Romans made their headquarters in the city of Olisipo. Today, this city is known as Lisbon, the capital of Portugal. The Romans brought many changes to Portugal. They built great roads and bridges and were a strong influence on the

A Roman bridge spans a valley

development of the Portuguese culture. Among Roman contributions was the introduction of Latin, which is the basis for the modern Portuguese language. They introduced the Christian religion too.

By the fifth century, the Romans had been pushed out by Germanic peoples. This group lived in communities that were widely scattered across the land. One of the cities of this time was called Cale. Today it is known as Oporto, an important port at the mouth of the Douro River in the north. The city became known as *Portucale*, meaning "the port of Cale." This is where the name Portugal came from.

At the beginning of the eighth century, a new kind of army invaded the peninsula. This was the Moors, a Muslim army from North Africa, and its mission was to take more land and to spread the religion of Islam, which had begun in Arabia in the seventh century.

The Muslims swept across Iberia and within five years had conquered the entire peninsula. Their rule lasted for 250 years. During that time they contributed enormously to Portuguese society and culture. They built schools and libraries, and shared their scientific knowledge, which was much more advanced than that of Europeans at the same time. Only the extreme northwest of the country, known as the Minho, remained under the influence of the Catholic Church. It was this region that strongly resisted converting to Islam. When the Muslims began to fight among themselves for a larger share of the territory, they lost control over the region.

Their religion lost its power too. The first blows against the Muslims came from the Catholic north, and battles there were fierce as each side fought for its beliefs. At this time, people were often converted from one religion to another with very little opposition. Few people were literate so they did not read the holy books—the Bible and the Koran, the Muslim holy book. When we say that a region became Muslim and then became Catholic, it means that the rulers and the educated people of the day followed those religions. They then claimed that the entire region followed the same religion.

Alfonso Henriques ruled Portugal's first kingdom.

Wars were often fought in the name of religion, however, and when the people protested against the rule of the Moors, they were also protesting against their religion. Long before there was such a thing as a Portuguese nation, the Roman Catholic Church was established. The first king of Portugal, Alfonso Henriques, used the support of the church to unify Portugal. He did so by granting church authorities large pieces of land.

The Christians reclaimed Portugal in the tenth century. These conquests were led by the Spanish kingdoms of Leon and Castile. The Spanish king Alfonso VI appointed Henry of Burgundy as count of Portugal in 1095. In the early part of the twelfth century, his son, Alfonso Henriques, began calling himself King Alfonso I. This was the beginning of Portugal's first kingdom. Alfonso Henriques waged wars against the Muslims, reconquering lost territory, and by 1270 had established most of the present boundaries of Portugal.

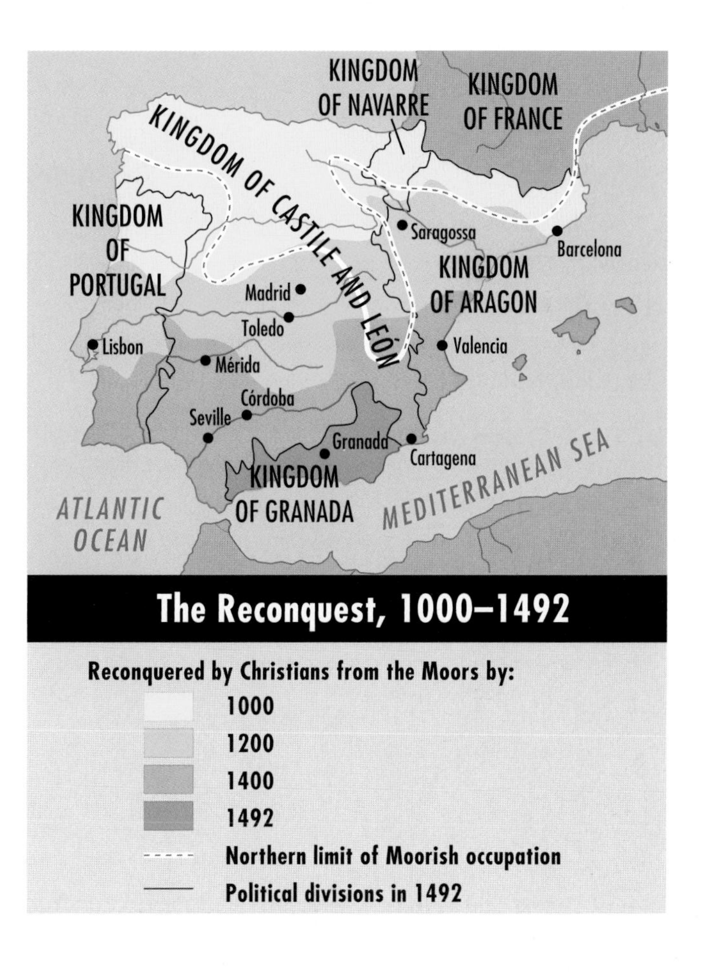

The Reconquest, 1000–1492

Throughout this time, and for another two centuries, internal struggles for control of the Portuguese government continued. The rulers wanted to protect their territory and spread their influence. Their opponents were wealthy nobles who also wanted power, especially the power to collect taxes and make decisions about legal matters. Once the Portuguese had stopped fighting among themselves, they turned their attention to the outside world.

At the beginning of the fifteenth century, Portuguese explorers began to sail the oceans beyond their own shores. Sailors traveled south, following the coastline of west Africa. As they made their way around the great western "bump" of Africa, they landed briefly and left stone markers and forts. The markers proved that the sailors had actually reached these distant points. The forts were needed to protect future Portuguese explorers who tried to gain control of the lands

The Astrolabe

When the sailors set out from Portugal, they had no scientific methods of navigation. Most sailors of the time hugged the shoreline, staying in sight of land. But when they ventured farther out to sea and lost sight of the land, they had very little to guide them. The instrument that allowed the Portuguese sailors to move about the oceans of the world with such confidence was the mariner's astrolabe.

This simple instrument permitted the sailors to measure latitude. Latitude is an imaginary line drawn around the globe that describes a position north or south of the equator. The sailor would take measurements using the position of the sun and the stars and then calculate the position of the ship. By sailing along a "line of latitude" the ship could be guided to a specific location—and return to that location. An astrolabe for astronomers had been in use for 1,000 years. The mariner's version used by the Portuguese enabled them to sail beyond the limits of traditional navigation techniques.

they reached in Africa. The peoples who lived along the coastline naturally saw these new arrivals as invaders. The first goal of these voyages was to spread Christianity around the world and to find a sea route to India.

Portuguese Travel the World

By the fifteenth and sixteenth centuries, the Portuguese had reached distant points around the world. Wherever they went, they claimed the land—and the people living on it—for Portugal. They sailed to the isolated islands of Madeira and the Azores, both located hundreds of miles southwest of Portugal. Madeira was not populated when they reached it. They also sailed to the Cape Verde Islands, many hundreds of miles farther out in the Atlantic Ocean. The Portuguese sailed as far as the eastern coast of South America where they

claimed the territory of Brazil for the Portuguese king. This became Portugal's largest colony. The Portuguese built up an empire of colonies. They also set the stage for their major role in the slave trade.

Portuguese explorers arrive on the coast of South America.

The Portuguese had control or influence along the entire western coast of Africa from the extreme northwestern point, all the way south around the Cape of Good Hope and up

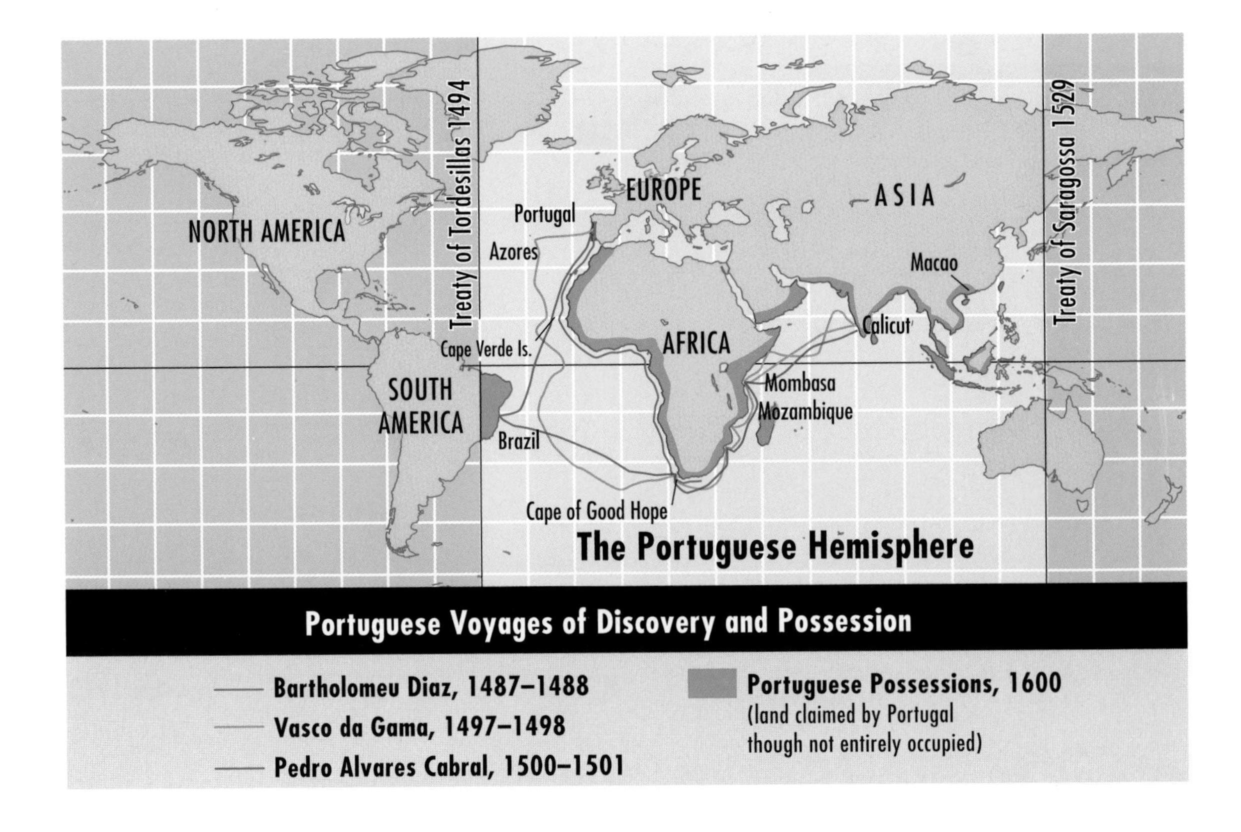

along the eastern coast of Africa, to the Red Sea. They continued on to the Indian subcontinent where they established outposts along the west coast of India and then moved eastward, claiming stretches of China, the Malacca Peninsula, Sumatra, Java, Timor, and the Cebes Islands. They even established a colony at Macao on the southeast coast of China.

Belém Tower

In the early 1500s, the Portuguese built a fortress on the shore of the Tagus River. Called the Tower of Belém, the fortress became a navigation point from which Portuguese explorers set out. The tower has stone carvings of rope and a watchtower as well as battlements formed like shields. Prisons built under the main terrace were cold, damp, and dreary. Today, the Tower of Belém gives visitors a look into the nation's history.

It would be another 500 years—the year 2000—before Macao lost its status as a Portuguese colony.

The Portuguese sailed steadily southward along the African coast until they could turn to the East. The search for a route to the lands that produced spices was one of the most important forces driving these early explorations. Spices preserved foods and, in the days before refrigeration, they were a main way to be sure of keeping food safe to eat. We think of spice as something extra added to food for flavor, but for the early Europeans, spice could mean survival.

King João I

King João I ruled for nearly fifty years—from 1385 to 1433. Under his rule, Portuguese sailors began to explore the seas and travel to distant lands. Their goals were mainly economic. The king's sons—Duarte, Pedro, Henry, Fernão, and João—were part of his ruling group and were called the "marvelous generation" by poet Luis de Camões. His son Henry, who became known as Henry the Navigator, was head of the Order of Christ, a military-religious order. King João wanted to find new lands in order to increase trade. Overseas exploration stopped briefly after he died but then was resumed under King Alfonso and João II. These early explorations had mixed goals. While the search for spices was always important, many of the sailor-explorers were sent to fight and kill Muslims. This gave missions, such as the Crusades, a religious aspect. And like the Crusades, these missions reflected a very cruel part of Portugal's history.

Henry the Navigator

Prince Henry, one of João I's sons, became known as Henry the Navigator. Although he was not a sailor himself, in 1418 he established a school of navigation in Sagres, a town on the western edge of Portugal. Prince Henry had the financial backing of the Catholic religious sect, the Order of Christ, so he was able to provide the money to support these expensive voyages. Prince Henry also had scientific curiosity, a desire to know what could be found in distant lands. He held strong religious beliefs and felt that these voyages would help spread Christianity and stop the growing influence of Islam. Prince Henry believed that if the sailors traveled around the coast of Africa, they would arrive at India. At each step along the way, he established the Portuguese presence.

When the first slaves were brought back from Africa, the Portuguese saw them as a source of wealth. Most of this wealth was limited to members of the court and the rich merchants of Portugal. Almost none of it was used to benefit the Portuguese people. In 1443, a Portuguese ship reached the coast of the country we now know as Mauritania. Immediately, a base was set up to begin shipping Africans to the Caribbean where they were used as unpaid laborers on plantations.

The slave trade changed the African continent forever. It robbed some villages of the strongest and most productive people. It provided the financing for wars between tribes in Africa. It turned some African chiefs into slavers who sold their own people or people from other tribes to the slave traders. The slave trade changed the economy and the populations of Brazil and the region that would become the United States of America. Without slaves, the plantations of the American South would not have developed as quickly as they did, nor would they have been so profitable. The slave traders also dragged Angolans and Mozambicans from their homes and robbed Portugal of many of its best people. Many of them never returned from the distant Portuguese settlements. Also, the wealth that was created from slavery was needed to guard those faraway settlements.

By the time Prince Henry died in 1460, Portuguese sailors had traveled as far south along the African coast as the country of Sierra Leone. They had also reached and claimed the islands of Madeira, the Azores, and the Cape Verde Islands.

The Caravel

The kind of ship that carried Portuguese explorers around the world is called a caravel. The caravel was an elegant, large vessel that curved to a point. It carried three masts with large square sails. It was on such a boat that Bartolomeu Dias made his trip around the Cape of Good Hope in 1488. The seaworthiness of these ships was demonstrated by the success of the men who sailed them. In 1987, a replica of Dias's ship was built and sailed from Lisbon, Portugal, to Mossel Bay, South Africa. Dias left Portugal in August 1487 and reached Mossel Bay in February 1488. The trip on the newly built caravel marked the 500th anniversary of that voyage. It took three months, half as long as it took Dias. The new caravel was then permanently docked inside the Bartolomeu Dias Museum in Mossel Bay. It is a grand sight, made entirely of pine and oak, with gleaming brass fittings. The crew of the new caravel included ten Portuguese and seven South Africans. Three of the South Africans were of Portuguese descent.

The Explorers

Although many brave sailors were responsible for Portugal's explorations, two names stand out. Bartolomeu Dias (1450–1500) was the first sailor to travel the length of Africa's west coast, around the Cape of Good Hope, and then up around the east coast of Africa into the Indian Ocean. His journey in 1487–1488 was the first step in Portugal's journey to the east. Dias was followed by Vasco da Gama (1460–1524). Da Gama also sailed around the Cape of Good Hope and then continued along the east coast of Africa. Finally, in 1498, sailing to the northeast, he made his way to India. This was the goal of the Portuguese and many other Europeans of the time. This also led to some of Portugal's smallest, and most distant colonies, including Goa, Malacca, Ormuz, and Macao. Portugal held on to some of these colonies for more than 500 years. The local people in each of these regions were forced to live under Portuguese rulers.

The Portuguese Empire

When Portugal's explorers set sail, they had three goals: to find a better route to the lands of spices in the east, to spread the Christian religion, and to gain more territory. That third goal would lead to tiny Portugal's role as a major colonial power. When Portugal's sailors set out to explore the world's oceans, looking for spices, they made a number of "discoveries" along the way. We call these finds "discoveries" because they were unknown at the time to people living in Europe. They were, of course, well known to the people who already lived in these lands. Most of them were already inhabited when the Portuguese arrived but, like all the other colonial powers, the Portuguese didn't ask the local people if they wanted to be part of a Portuguese empire. They simply staked a claim and colonized the territories. Among the uninhabited islands reached by the Portuguese were the Madeira Islands and the Azores archipelago.

From tiny to enormous, Portugal's colonies stretched around the world. Among the tiniest are the Cape Verde Islands in the Atlantic Ocean, about 350 miles (560 km) west of Africa. No one lived on these isolated islands when Dinís Dias became the first Portuguese to land there in 1444. Portuguese farmers and sailors settled nine of the larger islands in the group. Then, because they needed more workers to farm the land, they forced people from West Africa to work as slaves. In some colonies, the Africans were forced to pay taxes in cash. The only way to earn cash was to work for the Portuguese.

The Portuguese often married people from West Africa and gave birth to children who were known as *mesticos*. These mixed-race people combined Portuguese culture and appearance with the culture and appearance of the Angolans and Mozambicans. The Portuguese mixed with the people they colonized more than other European powers did.

As the Portuguese explored farther down the west coast of Africa, King Alfonso V gave them financial encouragement. In the West African area we now know as Guinea, the king "gave" explorer Fernão Gomes the exclusive right to all the trade if Gomes agreed to continue exploring the coast. Gomes had to agree to explore a stretch of the coast equal to about 310 miles (500 km) each year. To prove they were actually covering new ground every year, the explorers left stone markers, built forts, and established trading stations. The Portuguese did not consider the rights of the people living there. They did not even think that the people living there had any rights.

Sailing farther south than any ships had gone before, Portuguese sailors made their way around the Cape of Good Hope and the southern tip of Africa. When Vasco da Gama landed at a point on the east coast of southern Africa on Christmas Day 1497, he named the area Natal, because it marked the birthday of Christ.

Vasco da Gama

Vasco da Gama (1460?–1524) was born in Sines, Portugal, and learned astronomy and navigation. He served as an officer in the Portuguese Navy around the time that Columbus sailed to the Western Hemisphere. Da Gama followed the route of Bartolomeu Dias around the Cape of Good Hope, Africa, and located a route to India. Upon his return to Portugal, King Manuel awarded da Gama the title of Admiral of the Sea of India. In 1524, King John III named da Gama viceroy of India. He set sail to India and died shortly after his arrival in that country.

A *Distant Outpost*

The Portuguese reached the island of Timor in southeast Asia in 1512. It became a Portuguese colony in 1642 when troops established a trading post there. The claims over the island were divided by the Portuguese, who took the eastern portion, and the Dutch, who ruled the western side. East Timor was settled at first by Roman Catholic missionaries and as a result, it remains mostly Catholic in a region that is almost entirely Muslim. Eventually, the Portuguese came to govern the island and traders came to make their deals. East Timor represented some of the worst aspects of Portuguese colonialism. Virtually nothing was done to improve the island or the lives of the people. The Portuguese built no roads and established no schools, they simply flew the Portuguese flag over the tiny possession. This was typical of the way they ruled all their colonies. For hundreds of years, the Portuguese in the home country did not protest about the way the colonized people were treated. In 1974, when the Portuguese empire collapsed, the Portuguese left East Timor entirely and Indonesian troops flooded in. The East Timorese had traded one unfortunate ruler for another. When the people voted "yes" in a referendum in 1999 that would lead to independence, Indonesian troops destroyed property, executed thousands of civilians, and left thousands of others to die of starvation and disease. The Portuguese finally became angry at this but it was too late to do anything to help the East Timorese. In Lisbon, people took to the streets in silent protest against this cruelty but their concern also was much too late for the people of East Timor. United Nations-sponsored elections in August 2001 established a new eighty-eight-seat Parliament to write a new constitution for Timor. Independence was slated for 2002.

Portuguese Reach Brazil

Five hundred years ago, on April 22, 1500, the Portuguese sailor Pedro Álvares Cabral arrived safely on the coast of South America, at a point he called *Porto Seguro*, which means "safe harbor." His arrival marked the beginning of Portugal's rule over its biggest colonial possession—Brazil. The huge territory remained a colony for more than 300 years, attaining

Portugal establishes its largest colony, Brazil.

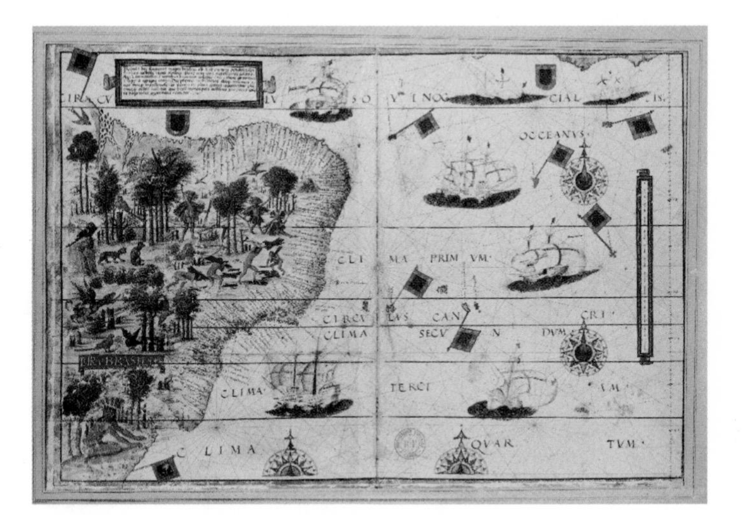

Cabral's Error

Born near Covilha, Portugal, Pedro Álvares Cabral (1467?–1528?) was one of Portugal's most famous explorers. In 1500, Cabral and thirteen ships sailed from Belém, headed toward the Cape of Good Hope. They set out to the southwest, were thrown off course, and sailed across the Atlantic to South America. There, Cabral claimed Brazil for Portugal. Scholars believe that he may have had no knowledge of navigation before leaving on this trip, which explains how Cabral's fleet could go so far off course. Cabral's "mistake" resulted in one of Portugal's most valued and valuable colonies.

independence in 1822. During that time, Portugal introduced the Portuguese language, still spoken in Brazil today, and established the borders of the territory. It also introduced slavery. Brazil was rich in gold and diamonds and Portugal profited from this colony. Today, with a population of 160 million, Brazil is the largest Portuguese-speaking country in the world and is the major reason Portuguese is the eighth most-spoken language in the world. However, most other regions of South America were colonized by Spain, so Brazil's neighbors are Spanish-speaking people.

Learning from Europe

King Manuel I, who ruled from 1495 to 1521, is credited with establishing formal, advanced education in Portugal. He reached out to the other European powers, and Portuguese men began to travel to Italy, France, and Spain to further their education. Portugal's close ties with Europe enabled it to take part in the great technological and cultural changes that were taking place in the region. During this period, individual Portuguese explorers set out on great travels, learning about the world and writing of their experiences. In 1487, even before Manuel I came to power, a printing press was established in Lisbon, so that these writings could be published there.

Portuguese Inquisition

When João III took over in 1521, ruling until 1557, he continued to expand Portugal's contacts with the world through trade. But he also created one of the darkest times in Portugal's history, the period known as the Inquisition. The Inquisition was first established in Spain in 1492 in order to get rid of anyone who did not believe in Christ. It was an effort by the Roman Catholic Church to end all opposition to its teachings. The Inquisition attacked not only non-Christians, but also those who converted to Christianity. The Inquisition became so powerful in Portugal that its members became the real rulers of the country, not the king.

The Inquisition Court executed those who did not believe in Christ.

When King Sebastian came to power in 1568, the Inquisition became even stronger. He was also intent on sending soldiers out on crusades against the Moors of North Africa. He spent so much money on wars that he bankrupted the country. Portugal became so weak that Spain's King Philip II was able to invade and conquer Portugal in 1580. Portugal was ruled by a Spanish king as part of the Iberian Union until 1640. The Portuguese finally rebelled and re-established their own monarchy. The Duke of Bragança became King João IV under the House of Bragança, which remained in power until 1910.

During one period in the 1700s, the little country became very wealthy, thanks to gold and diamonds discovered in the colony of Brazil. This wealth was spent by King João V who built palaces, churches, and monasteries. In 1750, he was followed by his son José, who had little interest in ruling. José turned over most of the power to the Marquês de Pombal. The Inquisition was formally abolished in 1821 when a new constitution was written.

Brazil Becomes Independent

During the late 1700s and early 1800s, the major regions of Europe fought a series of wars to try to claim economic power over greater regions. Portugal and its monarchy were so weakened that the capital city was actually moved all the way across the Atlantic Ocean to Rio de Janeiro in Brazil. With Portugal so weak, the Brazilians demanded their own kingdom. The king's son, John, who was ruling Brazil, liked his life there and agreed to their demands. In 1822, Brazil became independent—a huge financial loss for Portugal.

The African Colonies

Portugal next turned to the exploration of its African colonies. Although it claimed huge territories in Africa, most of Portugal's contacts were limited to the coastal regions. This was also true of the other colonial powers that had made claims over various parts of Africa. In most cases, the regions were unknown and uncharted by the Europeans who staked claims to them. Portugal thought of its colonies as places to exploit natural resources such as gold and ivory, and to expand agriculture. It used the Angolans, Mozambicans, and Guineans as slave labor. At the same time, its claim on these territories was disputed by other European countries.

In order to settle these claims, and establish boundaries between the various parts of Africa, the European powers met in Berlin, Germany, in 1884–1885 to divide up Africa

The Conference at Berlin was held to discuss European territorial claims in Africa.

among themselves. No Africans took part at this meeting. The Europeans agreed that Portugal could claim the territories of Mozambique, Angola, and Guinea. A map was drawn showing the regions each nation claimed. Portugal's claims were shown in red, which became known as the "rose-colored map." The rose-colored map claimed all the territory between Mozambique and Angola, which included the country of South Africa. The British refused to even discuss this conflicting claim and sent an ultimatum to Portugal, demanding that Portuguese forces withdraw from this territory. The Portuguese knew they could not hope to match the power of the British, so they withdrew. This event set the stage for the end of the monarchy in Portugal.

A group known as "Republicans" were afraid that Portugal's government had become so weak that it could easily be taken over by another European power. Portugal's colonies had proven to be very expensive. Instead of money flowing into the treasury, it was flooding out to defend the colonies. The government was determined to hold onto the colonies, though. They were a vital part of Portugal's belief that it was one of the super-powers of its day and they also gave Portugal territory around the world. Carlos I even tried to expand the African colonies during his reign, from 1889–1908. In 1892, Portugal actually declared bankruptcy. The end of the monarchy was near. In 1908, Carlos was assassinated along with his son, who would have become the next king. Manuel II then became king.

The First Republic

In 1910, an effort was made to save the monarchy, but it failed. The monarchy had become too weak to survive. The Republicans grew stronger and forced elections for a new form of government called the First Republic. This was not a peaceful time for Portugal. The nation had forty-five governments between 1910 and 1926, with governments falling almost as fast as they took office. Its weak economy was at the heart of Portugal's problems. No government could make the people's lives better without money. Military leaders would seize power, and then be defeated by democratic forces, in a process that kept repeating itself. In 1922, General Manuel Gomes da Costa marched into Lisbon with his troops and took control of the government. There was no opposition, so the takeover was called a bloodless coup, a word that means a "blow." The most important change came in 1928 when the military named António de Oliveira Salazar as minister of finance. Salazar soon became the real leader of the government. By 1932, he was appointed prime minister. Salazar ruled Portugal with an iron hand. He banned political parties and ruled with a close circle of his own friends, turning Portugal into a dictatorship. He did not trust the Portuguese people to make good decisions, so he took more and more power for himself. To keep people happy, they were urged to participate in three approved activities—music, religion, and sports.

Salazar Era

The dictatorship of António de Oliveira Salazar lasted until 1968. Salazar was successful in running the country's finances.

António de Oliveira Salazar

Born in the small Portuguese village of Santa Comba Dão, António de Oliveira Salazar (1889–1970) was a lawyer and an economist. In 1926, Salazar, then teaching at Coimbra University, was asked to help solve the economic problems of Portugal. From 1932 to 1968 he ruled Portugal with an iron hand and supported his dictatorship by use of secret police. During his reign as dictator, Salazar controlled the police, the military, labor unions, banks, and schools. Portuguese citizens were denied political freedom, as well as freedom of speech. In 1968, Salazar suffered a serious stroke, which left him unable to continue as prime minister. He died in Lisbon two years later.

Although he was able to reduce Portugal's debt, most of the people lived in dreadful poverty. Portugal was often called "the poor man of Europe." His policies kept the nation from developing and growing. He also kept Portugal segregated from the rest of Europe—and the world. In every way, he held onto old ways. He ignored technological advances as well as ways to improve education and even improvements in farming that would have helped the Portuguese out of their poverty. Because he was deeply religious, he encouraged the people to strengthen their beliefs in Catholicism. He also fought to hold onto the colonies at a time when all the other European powers were granting independence to their colonies. With their colonies, the Portuguese believed that they were a great nation; without them, Portugal was just a small, unimportant country. The colonies continued to drain

Portugal's economy, especially as the people in these distant lands began to rise up against the Portuguese. But the Portuguese were not allowed to criticize any of Salazar's actions. Newspapers, books, and art were censored. Nothing negative was allowed to be said about the government.

World War II

During World War II (1939–1945), Portugal managed to avoid committing itself to either side and officially it was neutral. In fact, it helped both sides. While Portugal allowed Britain and the United States to use the Azores as military bases, it also supplied the Axis powers, including Nazi Germany, with a mineral needed for production of steel. Much of the economy of Portugal was supported by gold that Nazi Germany stole from the Jews before they were sent to the concentration camps. Lisbon remained an open city in many respects and served as a "listening post" for the rest of Europe.

After the war, Portugal kept a firm grip on its African colonies. It declared that Angola, Mozambique, and Guinea were "overseas provinces" and had the same status as the provinces of Portugal itself. Salazar suffered a stroke in 1968 and his thirty-six-year iron grip on Portugal ended. Power then shifted to Marcello Caetano who ruled Portugal until 1974.

The African Wars

During the 1960s and into the 1970s, the people of Angola, Mozambique, and Guinea-Bissau began to revolt against their Portuguese rulers. As these uprisings grew in strength, the

African children sit on a statue that was thrown over during the civil war in Angola.

Portuguese sent more and more troops to maintain control. A great deal of money went to fighting in the "overseas provinces."

Resistance in Portugal took the form of emigration. People did not see a future for themselves in Portugal and they grew very tired of sending their sons off to die in wars in order to hold on to distant African lands. The Portuguese believed that these distant "citizens" really were Portuguese. If that was so, how could they kill them just to maintain control over their territory?

Revolution of the Carnations

The answer is, "They couldn't." The military itself saw the need for a change in direction and a change in government. In 1973, soldiers formed the Armed Forces movement. Then, in 1974, General António de Spinola published a book calling for a military takeover of the government. The end was in sight.

On April 25, 1974, a military group seized control of the government. Using a prearranged signal, they played a song called *Grandola, Vila Morena* on the radio to signal that they were ready. The troops took over key points throughout Lisbon and all over the countryside. This became known as the Revolution of the Carnations because the people took to the streets and put red carnations into the barrels of the soldiers' rifles.

Portuguese soldiers display carnations as the symbol of liberation.

Colonies Are Set Free

Almost immediately after the April 25 revolution, plans were set into motion to finally let the African colonies go their own ways. Rapidly, Portugal gave independence to Guinea-Bissau, Mozambique, the Cape Verde Islands, São Tomé, and Angola. But the colonies had not been prepared for independence. There were virtually no Angolan doctors, Mozambican teachers, or any of the other professionals needed to run a modern nation. Samora Machel, who became the president of Mozambique, said that Portugal left them with no trained personnel to take over.

There was no history of elections and there were different factions who wanted to rule. It was clear to the Portuguese who had been living in these countries that wars were about to erupt. Many fled to Portugal. This left the new African countries without the people who had been running their government institutions and basic services. The colonies suffered greatly, and continue to suffer today from this abrupt departure. In one colony, it was said that the Portuguese left so quickly that they didn't even take the time to lower the

Refugees show their papers upon arrival in Lisbon.

Portuguese flag. Many Angolans left the country too, choosing a future in Portugal. The total number is estimated at about 350,000–500,000.

The Second Republic

Portugal's Second Republic began on the day of the revolution, April 25, and continues today. Portugal has been a democratically ruled nation for only a little more than a quarter-century. It has gone through a number of governments, trying out a Socialist leader and then a more capitalist type of government.

Perhaps the most remarkable achievement has been the successful integration of all the refugees. Many Angolans who had been government employees, working for the Portuguese, were given jobs in Portugal. Others worked in construction, for utility companies, in the school system, and as shopkeepers. Many were given government subsidies to set up small businesses. They were known for their ability in such fields as maintenance and automobile repair.

Women's Rights

It wasn't until after the Revolution of 1974 that women gained equal rights in Portugal. The 1933 constitution gave everyone in Portugal equal rights, "except for women." Throughout history, Portuguese women were obliged by law to follow the dictates of their fathers and husbands. They could neither own property nor vote. A new constitution, passed in 1976, gave women full legal rights. In 1991, a Commission for Equality and Women's Rights was formed to improve the position of women in Portuguese society and protect their rights.

Today, women doctors and lawyers account for two out of five professional people in Portugal. More than half of all Portuguese people attending colleges and universities are women. Although women still do not earn equal pay for equal jobs, many more jobs are now open to women, including employment in offices and factories.

Mário Soares, the Socialist Party leader, was named prime minister in 1976. Although his party lost power in 1977, he was elected president in 1986 and reelected in 1991. The party that gained power was the Social Democrats, who favored capitalism. Anibal Cavaco Silva, their leader, was successful in modernizing Portugal's economy. Many industries and businesses had been taken over by the government during the Salazar years and were quite inefficient. Silva returned them to private ownership and the kind of competition that helps keep companies profitable.

This change in the economy allowed Portugal to shake off its old "poor man" image. In 1986, it joined the European Community, also known as the European Union, a group of European nations that are working to become one economic unit, like the United States. This membership is probably the most important indication that Portugal intends to compete with the most industrialized and modern countries in the world.

CHAPTER FIVE

Ruling Portugal

Portugal has three branches of government—executive, legislative, and judicial. In the executive branch, the country is ruled by a president, known as the chief of state, and a prime minister, who is the head of government. The president is elected for a five-year term and presides over the Council of State. He also appoints the prime minister, who is usually the leader of the majority party. Although he is appointed and not elected, the prime minister is more important and powerful than the president. The president may not serve more than two terms. The president appoints the members of the Council of Ministers but he usually follows the recommendation of the prime minister.

Opposite: **Oporto town hall and gardens**

The exterior of Portugal's parliament building in Lisbon

The Council of State includes the president of the Assembly, the prime minister, the chief justices of the Supreme Court, and the members of the Constitutional Tribunal. Also included are the presidents of the regional governments and all former presidents of the republic. Ten citizens are included—five of them appointed by the president and five selected by the Assembly.

NATIONAL GOVERNMENT OF PORTUGAL

Executive

President or Chief of State

Prime Minister

Council of State

Council of Ministers (13)

Legislative

Assembly of the Republic

Judiciary

Supreme Court

Courts of Second Instance

Courts of First Instance

Regional Courts

Local Courts

Judiciary

The judiciary includes district courts, known as Courts of First Instance, courts of appeal, known as Courts of Second Instance, and the Supreme Court. There is a 13-member Constitutional Tribunal. The president rules on the constitutionality of laws.

Legislature

The legislative branch consists of a one-house body known as the Assembly of the Republic, with 240 to 250 members who are elected once every four years. Portugal also has twenty-two administrative divisions known as districts. Three of these are on the Azores and one is on Madeira. These islands have a measure of self-government but are still considered

Lisbon: Did You Know?

Located on the Tagus River, the capital city of Lisbon is known as the "town of the seven hills." The steep hills lead up to panoramic views of the city. The best view is from the Castelo de São Jorge, on the hill above the ancient Alfama district. This castle dates back to the fifth century A.D., and attests to the claim of Lisbon as one of the oldest cities in Europe.

Lisbon mingles the ancient and the modern, Roman and Moorish. Some of the sidewalks are paved with hand-cut cobblestones. The city proper has about 680,000 residents, with many thousands more living in the suburbs. The weather is pleasant, with warm summers and mild winters.

Portugal's nautical history is remembered through the Portuguese Navigators and Discoverers Monument, as well as at the Park of the Nations on the site of Expo '98.

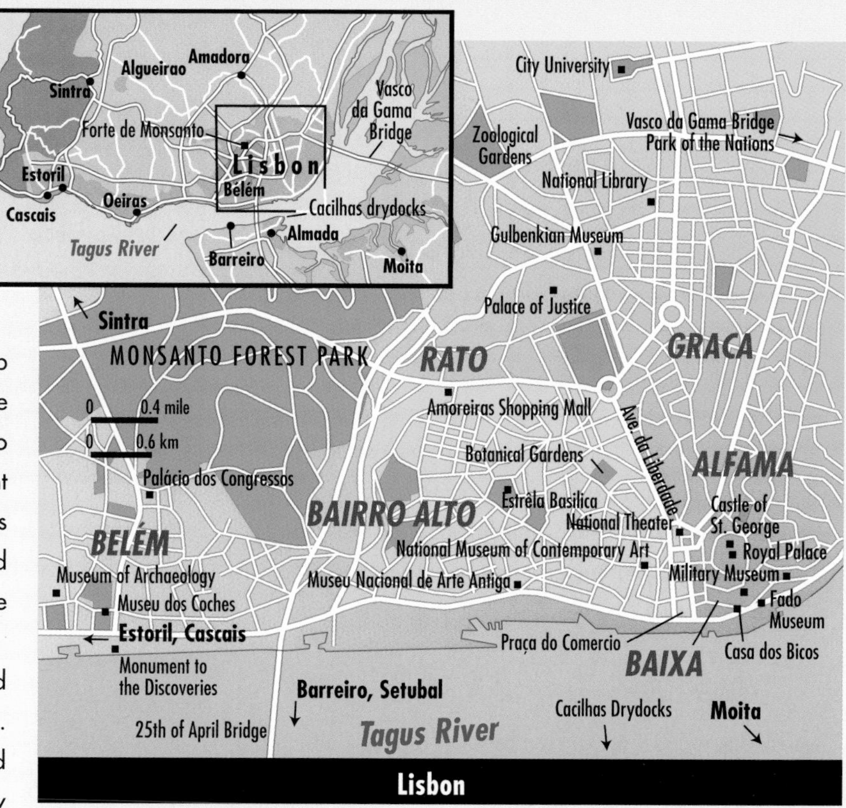

Lisbon

The Flag

Portugal's colorful flag was adopted after the revolution of 1910. The flag features two bold blocks of green and red with a large coat-of-arms symbol on the dividing line between the two color blocks. The green portion takes up two-fifths of the flag and the red occupies three-fifths. The green represents hope while the red reflects the courage and blood of the Portuguese who have died fighting for their country. The coat of arms combines blue and white shields that stand for many aspects of Portuguese history, especially King Alfonso Henriques's battles. The dots within the shields represent the role of Jesus Christ in the history of the nation. The navigators and the world they discovered are represented by a yellow sphere.

Mário Soares

Mário Soares is Portugal's most popular political figure. He was the country's first civilian president, elected in 1986 after five decades of dictatorship. He studied in Portugal at the University of Lisbon and also at the law school of the Sorbonne in Paris, where he became a student activist. His opposition to dictatorship brought him great hardship. He was jailed twelve times and sent into exile twice. After the revolution of 1974, he became foreign minister and was put in charge of negotiations leading to independence for the Portuguese colonies. He became the first constitutionally elected prime minister before being elected president. The constitution was amended several times. Subsequently, the president appoints the prime minister. He has remained an active and popular figure in Portugal's political life.

part of Portugal even though they are located in the Atlantic Ocean, hundreds of miles from the mainland.

The districts are composed of municipalities and further divided into parishes. About 4,000 parishes bring the government down to the local level throughout the country.

Portuguese president Jorge Sampaio (right) and Chinese president Jiang Zemin at the meeting to discuss Macao.

The Last Colony

On December 20, 1999, the Portuguese flag was lowered in Macao, the last colony under its control. Macao, a tiny piece of land on the very edge of China was thus turned over to Chinese control, ending 442 years of Portuguese rule. Portuguese sailors first landed on the territory in 1557. The turnover of control to China was so important that Portugal's president, Jorge Sampaio, joined the president of China, Jiang Zemin, for the occasion. He wanted to remind China that Portugal still felt responsible for the people of Macao.

Earning a Living

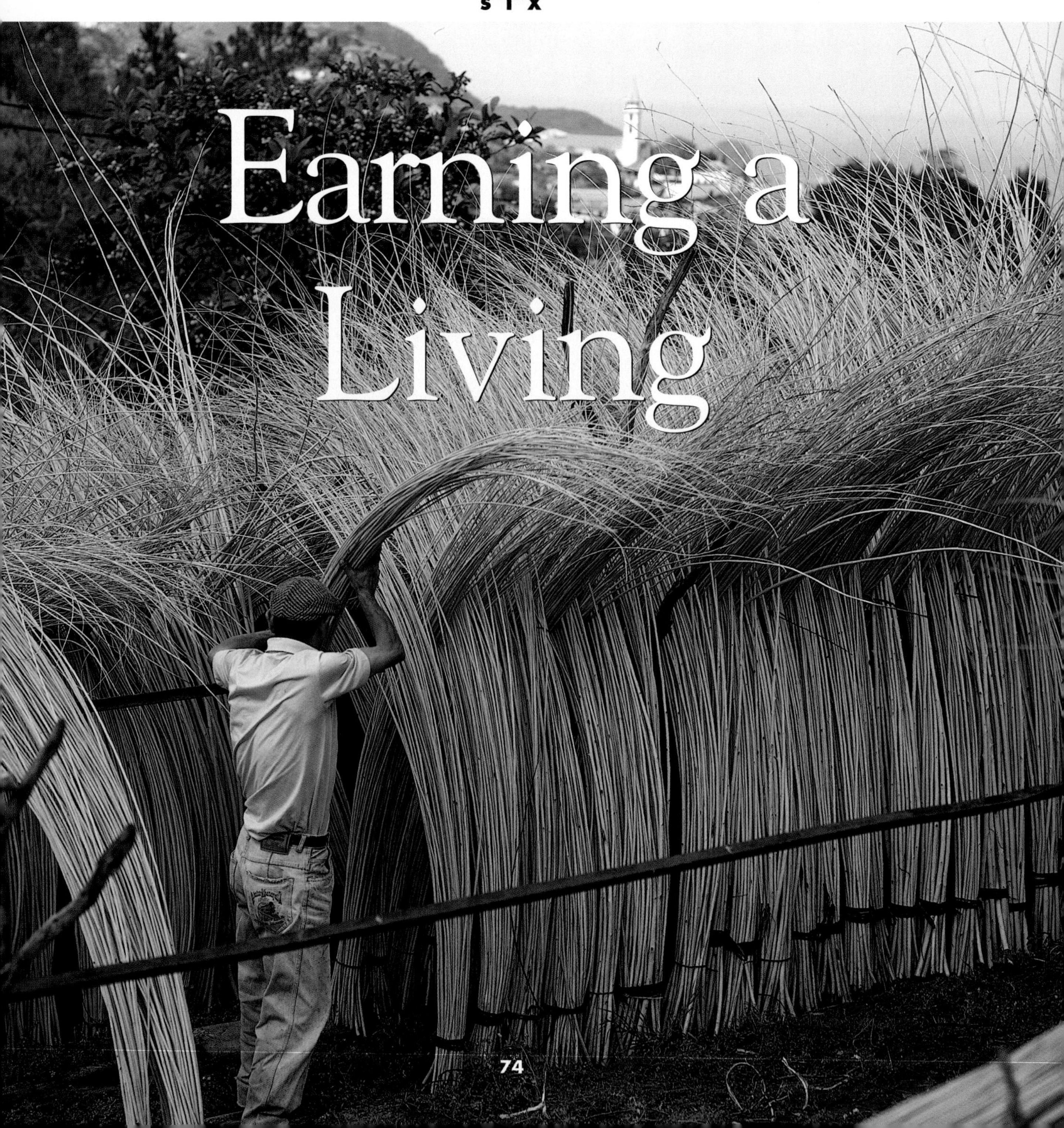

Opposite: **Raw willow bundles being dried in Madeira.**

Portugal's economy, which was at a standstill after the long Salazar dictatorship, is now a lively mix of traditional and modern industries. It has made giant leaps toward catching up to the rest of Europe since it became part of the European Union (EU) on January 1, 1986. The nation has been helped financially by the EU, which believes that every nation in the group should be on an equal footing. The traditional areas of agriculture, forestry, and fishing still employ nearly half the workers of Portugal.

A fisherman prepares his net for the daily catch.

Fishing

With its long coastline and seagoing tradition, it is natural that fishing is still an important part of Portugal's economy. Fish are at the heart of the Portuguese diet. The most popular fish are sardines, anchovies, tuna, and cod. In Nazaré, the men fish for sardines from small boats launched right into the ocean and return each night with their catch. In the Algarve region, and around the Azores, they catch tuna. In the fishing ports near

Fish for sale at the central market in Lisbon.

Oporto and Setubal, the fishermen go out into the deep waters of the ocean on large wooden trawlers called *traineiras*. They fish for cod, which is the favorite fish in the Portuguese diet. It is the main ingredient in the national dish, *bacalhau*. Today, because the waters around Portugal have been overfished, some of the fishermen wander far from their home port in search of cod—as far as the Grand Banks of Newfoundland in Canada. The boats measure about 32–80 feet (10–25 m) long. The traineiras bear a close resemblance to the caravels that Portuguese sailors used in the past to travel the oceans. These trips begin in the spring and take the men thousands of miles from home. They return in late summer with their holds completely filled with codfish. To preserve the fish during the long journey, it is salted and then stored.

In an effort to ensure the survival of the cod, the EU has set limits on the amount of fish that can be caught. Even with these limits, currently 48,600 tons a year, the officials are afraid that the species will die out.

What Portugal Grows, Makes, and Mines

Agriculture (1977)	
Potatoes	1,400,000 metric tons
Grapes	1,240,000 metric tons
Tomatoes	1,020,000 metric tons
Manufacturing (1994, ***value added in escudos*****)**	
Petroleum refining	361,511,000
Machinery and transport equipment	356,941,000
Wearing apparel and footwear	301,942,000
Mining (1996)	
Salt	609,639 metric tons
Silver	111,459 metric tons
Zinc	95,900 metric tons

Fishing Boats

Manpower is the key to the fishing boats used in the rough waters off Portugal's shores. These boats are based on designs that may date back to the Phoenicians. The typical boat is about 16 feet (5 m) long with a high prow that ends in a distinctive point. The boats are often painted with an evil eye—a symbol that is meant to protect the fishermen and the boat from evil spirits.

The brightly painted boats and the fishermen have a rough time of it, from the moment the boats are launched. The North Atlantic is very rough and there are few ports along the northernmost coast. In order to launch the boats, the fishermen place tree trunks on the beach and then roll the boats over the tree trunks into the surf. Then the crews jump into

Fishermen launch their boat into the surf.

the boats and row them out to an area where fish are usually found. The men set out their nets or traps, depending on the kind of fish they're looking for. These crews may stay out fishing all night and then return in the morning. After the men bring in the catch, the *varinas* (fishwives) take over and sell the fish right on the beach.

Fishwives drying the day's catch directly on the beach.

Blessing of the Fleet

In Viana Do Castelo, in northern Portugal, a three-day festival is held each year before the Blessing of the Fleet. The first day of the feast features arts and crafts, and a parade with humorous floats. On the second day the parade is based on the Bible, to emphasize the importance of the Catholic religion. The third day features the history of the relationship between Portugal and Spain, its neighbor.

After the third day's parade and feasting, the main road from the town's Catholic church to the docks is closed. During the night, colored sawdust is used to create pictures and patterns on the road. The next morning, fishermen carry banners bearing the names of their boats to the church. A mass honors these fishermen and the local bishop blesses the ships. The whole city partakes of the feast that follows. The community hopes the blessing will protect the fishermen while they are out at sea.

Port of Lisbon

Many great capital cities grow up around rivers and Lisbon is a perfect example of this. It has the best natural port in Europe and is able to handle large oceangoing boats. Goods that

Oceangoing boats docked in the Port of Lisbon.

arrive here can also be transported upriver all the way into the heart of Europe. In addition to the working boats, the port is known for the Cacilhas drydocks, the largest in the world. A drydock is a place where a ship can be isolated in a kind of container. The seawater is then drained out and the bottom of the ship can be repainted and repaired more easily.

Traditional wooden boats, barco rabelo, are still being built as they were in the fifteenth century.

Boat Building

It's not surprising that a nation with a rich sailing history should also be a nation of boatbuilders. Portuguese boats are built for specific purposes. Some are used to carry barrels of wine, while others are used by fishermen or by people gathering reeds. The most popular design is the flat-bottomed boat known as *barco rabelo*, often seen around Oporto. This boat has square sails marked with the emblems of the firms that produce the city's most famous product—port wine. It has an ancient history too. Similar boats were made and

Barco rabelo await the annual race.

used during the times of the Romans, thousands of years ago. These sturdy boats were made for use on the Douro River, a very rough waterway. When the rains are heavy, the Douro becomes a raging river, and river travel is very dangerous.

Barco Rabelo

Although much of the need for boats to carry the wine disappeared when vehicles on roads took over transportation, barco rabelo are still seen and appreciated today. Their role has shifted to one of racing in annual competitions. The port-wine shipping firms sponsor these races as a way of promoting their product and helping to keep this great tradition alive. The rules of the competition include the way the boats are made. The builders must follow traditional methods of boatbuilding, and the boats must be fashioned from pine trees found along Portugal's north coast. The huge sails can measure up to 80 feet (24 m) long. The biggest boats require at least a dozen crew members.

Young Portuguese cadets still train for the sea on the beautiful wooden ship called the *Sagres*. The *Sagres* now travels the world on goodwill missions. It came to New York in the year 2000 to take part in the international Op-Sail millennium event. It docked at the South Street Seaport where many Portuguese-Americans visited and talked to the Portuguese seamen.

Agriculture

Farming in Portugal is still a family business. Farms in northern Portugal are among the smallest in Europe. It is almost impossible to make such small farms more productive. A farmer working just 1 or 2 acres (0.4 or 0.8 hectares) can't afford to buy a modern tractor or other farm machinery that would increase the yield. Before 1975, much of the farmland in the south was owned by absentee landlords, people who lived away from the land. Even though their properties were larger, the owners did not invest much in new equipment or in modernizing the methods used on the farms. This kept them from increasing their productivity.

Farmers on small pieces of land still use donkey-pulled plows to till their fields.

Olive trees cover the land and produce one of Portugal's most important products, olive oil.

About 20 percent of Portuguese people are involved in farming or fishing. Farmers grow food for their own use and also to sell to nearby markets. Because their production is small, the country has not developed the vast network of roads and refrigerated trucks needed to carry fresh food for hundreds of miles to major cities.

Farmers grow maize (corn), wheat, potatoes, vegetables, sunflowers, and some rice in irrigated fields. Olives are one of the nation's most important crops. Olives are used to make olive oil. Olive trees dot the land. About 1,235,521 acres (500,000 ha) are planted with olive trees, making Portugal one of the most important producers in Europe. Olive oil is used in cooking and is considered one of the healthiest kinds of oils. Sunflower seeds are also used to make cooking oil. Maize is a major crop, too, with about 445,000 to 494,000 acres (180,000 to 200,000 ha) planted each year, depending on the weather. If there is too much rain to plant winter

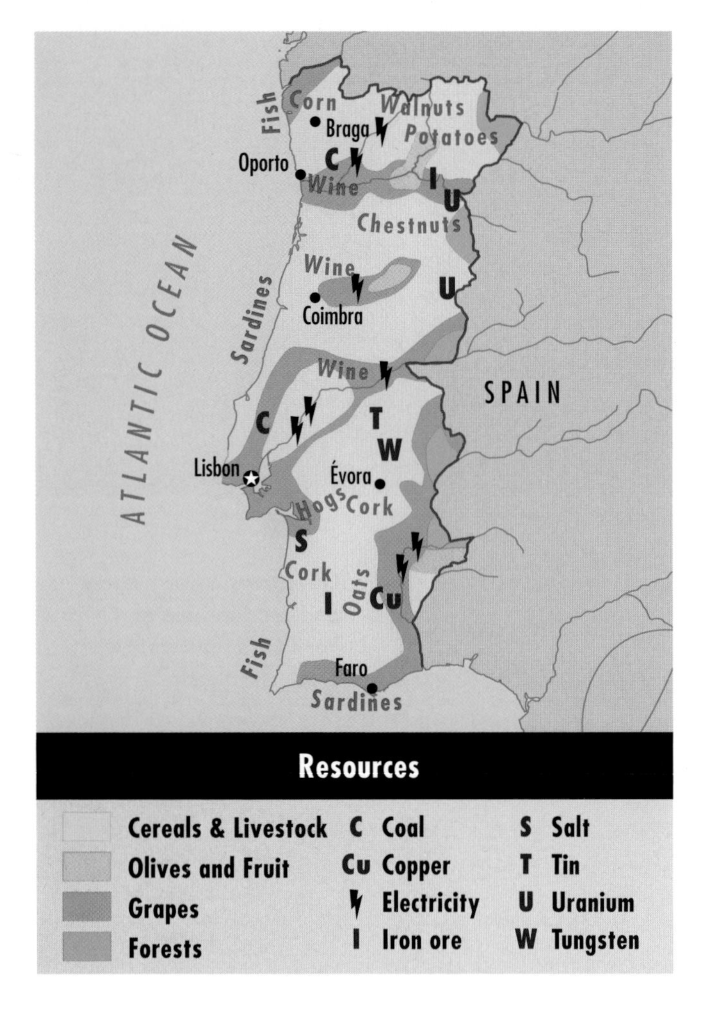

wheat, the farmers can plant maize instead. Even in a good year, Portugal must import maize to meet its needs. Most of the maize grown in Portugal is used as animal feed.

Wood Products

Trees are called a renewable resource because we can grow more trees to replace the ones we cut down. In Portugal, harvesting trees is a major industry. Portugal remains heavily wooded. About one-third of the land is forested and forest products are important to the economy. These include cork and resins as well as pine and eucalyptus timber. Pine is the principal tree used to make a wide range of household furniture. It is also used in construction, and other products such as turpentine are made from parts of the trees. Pine tree sap is used for resin. Trees are also used to make paper and cardboard. In addition to pine, Portugal uses eucalyptus trees for their oil and pulp.

Madeira

Madeira is famous for two products. The right combination of sun, soil, and rain produce a famous wine called Madeira. The grapes are grown on tiny bits of land that have been worked onto the steepest slopes of the islands. Madeira is also known for its unique embroidery, known as *bordados*, first introduced to the islanders by Elizabeth Phelps, an Englishwoman. This embroidery features open-work designs created by cutting out a lacy pattern in the fabric and then embroidering around the edges. Bordados is one of Madeira's most important cottage industries today.

Women embroider around open-work designs on the border of a tablecloth.

Cork Grows on Trees

Did you know that cork grows on trees? Cork is actually the bark of the cork oak. Cork oak trees are a very long-term investment for the farmer. From the time the oak begins to grow from a tiny acorn, it takes about twenty-five years until it can be used for its first crop of cork. Working only in the summer, farmers strip the outer layer of bark from the tree. This work must be done by hand because the trees are so irregular and machines would probably damage the tree by digging

A cork stripper peels away the cork from a cork oak.

Portuguese Currency

The traditional currency of Portugal has been the escudo. At the beginning of 2002, however, the Portuguese currency was changed to the euro, the currency used by most nations of the European Union. The Portuguese had just two months to hand over all their bills and coins, and receive euros in exchange. In order to get people used to the idea of the new currency, businesses had been posting prices in euros and escudos for more than two years. Portugal's old paper money (above) showed famous Portuguese explorers and was printed in bills ranging from 50 escudos to 2,000 escudos. In 2001, U.S.$1 was equal to about 175 to 190 escudos. For business people, using the same currency in Portugal, France, Germany, and other countries eliminates the need to figure exchange rates and handle different kinds of currency. It is easier for people traveling from one country to the other, too. Now, travelers will be able to use the same currency almost everywhere in Europe. The Portuguese have had more than a year to get used to seeing prices quoted in euros and escudos.

Euros are printed in seven different amounts—5, 10, 20, 50, 100, 200, and 500 euro notes. The same bills are used throughout the European Union. The designs are symbolic of European architecture but they do not show specific buildings. The fronts show windows and gateways while the reverse sides show a bridge. The coins (above) all have the same design on the front but each country can use its own design on the reverse. All the coins and bills may be used in any European Union country. Portugal has decided not to use the two larger bills, the 200- and 500-euro notes. They represent very large amounts of money. The 500-euro note is nearly equal to the average monthly salary in Portugal.

The Metric System

Portugal uses metric measurements.

in too deeply. A cork oak tree produces from 60 to 100 pounds (28 to 45 kg) of cork each time it is cut. Then the farmer must wait nine years before the bark grows back and the cork can be harvested again. In 2000, Portugal produced more than 150,000 tons (136,000 metric tons) of cork, more than half the world's production. This makes cork one of Portugal's most important products. Recently, plastic corks have been replacing natural cork in some wines but people who appreciate fine wines prefer natural cork. It has the unique ability to allow the wine to breathe while it ages in the bottle.

What Does it Cost?

Here are some common prices for items in Portugal.
U.S. prices are based on 188 escudos = $1.

Item	Price in Escudos	Price in U.S. currency
Mars candy bar	120	$0.63
Loaf of bread	150	$0.80
Soda	150	$0.80
Fast-food hamburger/fries	600	$3.19
Postage stamp	85	$0.45
Movie ticket	900	$4.79
Gasoline (1 liter)	165	$0.88 ($3.32/gallon)

Visiting Portugal

Tourism is the greatest single source of foreign exchange. Nearly 28 million foreigners entered Portugal in the year 2000, each staying an average of three nights. About 10 percent of the visitors come from the United States. The number of U.S. citizens traveling to Portugal has been increasing slowly. Most foreign visitors come from neighboring Spain; they can drive over the border and return home in one day. They don't contribute as much to the economy as visitors from the United Kingdom and Germany who fill up most hotel rooms and therefore spend more money.

Labor Force

Portugal's labor force numbers about 5 million workers. Women make up about 45 percent of the total workforce. More than 1 million Portuguese are self-employed. About 22 percent of the workforce is employed in manufacturing, while about 12 percent is in agriculture, which includes fishing and farming. People who provide personal services, such as waiters and hotel workers, make up another 22 percent of the workforce.

Portugal's Wines

For a small country, Portugal is a major wine producer. In 2000, Portugal made about 145 million gallons (549 million liters) of wine and exported 50 million gallons (189 million liters) of the total. In addition to port, it is also known for *Vinho Verde*, which means "green wine." That doesn't refer to the color, but to the age of the wine. It's meant to be consumed right after it's put in the bottle, unlike other wines, which improve with age.

An inspector evaluates wine as it ages.

Porcelain Dinnerware

Since 1824, Portugal has been producing beautiful porcelain dinnerware on a farm called *Vista Alegre*, which means "pleasant view," in the town of Ilhavo. The dinnerware is handmade, with talented local workers painting the floral designs and Moorish patterns directly on the pieces. The area, a four-hour drive north of Lisbon, is inspiring, and has always been the home of the factory. Vista Alegre has been in the same family since its founding and is the principal source of employment in the region. The local clay provides the basic material for the dinnerware but it is the skillful artists who turn it into a product that is exported to other European countries as well as the United States. Vista Alegre also creates patterns that are inspired by the Azueljos, the tiles that are seen everywhere you go, especially in Lisbon.

Dinnerware displaying hand-painted designs

Machines shape plates from huge rolls of clay in the Spal porcelain factory.

Spal is another dinnerware company that manufactures dishes by the thousands. Spal uses mass-production techniques and modern equipment. Machines slice up huge rolls of clay just as a baker slices up bread. Then the clay is baked and decorated. Much of the work is now done by machines.

Government Workers

About 600,000 people—more than 10 percent of the entire workforce—are employed by the government. The major areas of government employment are education (200,000) and health care (110,000). Local governments employ about 100,000 people.

Manufacturing

Portugal's economy includes many small manufacturing companies. About 600 factories are set up to manufacture textiles, clothing, and footwear. Small plants making medical equipment, vehicles, and furniture employ about 160,000 people. Automobiles are also assembled in Portugal. The European Community has invested substantially in Portugal to help the country modernize its industries. EDP, a company that provides electricity to Portugal's businesses and homes, employs 13,550 people. Most of the manufacturing companies are located around Lisbon and Oporto. Most of the trading in the manufactured products is with other European Union countries.

Mining

Portugal's mining industry began in 1979. Today, it is the biggest producer of tungsten ore in Europe. Portugal's mining company, Avocet Mining PLC, mines the mineral at the Panasqueira mine. It is located on the southern edge of the Serra da Estrela mountain range and workers are recruited from villages near the mine. Tungsten is an important mineral used in producing filaments for lightbulbs. It is also needed to harden steel. Portugal produced an estimated 826.7 tons (750 metric tons) of tungsten in 2000 and has reserves estimated at 25,000 tons (27,500 metric tons). Tungsten is a very valuable mineral. Portugal mines copper at Neves Corvo copper mine. In 1998, it mined 125,663 tons (114,000 metric tons) of copper. It also mined 4,409 tons (4,000 metric tons) of tin.

Traditionally, Portuguese who emigrate to other countries to find work send part of their earnings back to their families in Portugal. These workers, who live in other parts of western Europe, especially Paris, as well as in Brazil and in North America, are an important part of the Portuguese economy.

The Changing Face of Portugal

Opposite: **Two young faces of Portugal**

PORTUGAL'S POPULATION TOTALS ABOUT 10 MILLION, THE same number of people as in 1975. In the years since 1975, the population has fallen and then risen again. Many people left Portugal to find work in other countries. Their places were taken by a flood of refugees, mainly from Angola, when the colonies gained independence. In July 2000, the figure was 10,048,232. Portugal has a low birth rate, with each woman having an average of two children. In the past, families were larger.

One of the major reasons for this change is an increase in education and especially in literacy. The literacy rate is 90 percent although there is still a group of older adults, especially

Portugal's Ethnic Background

The vast majority of Portuguese people combine an ancient mix of Germanic, Iberian, Roman, Phoenician, Moorish, and Carthaginian background. However, all of it has come together to create the modern Portuguese. Most people have dark hair and dark brown eyes, and their skin color tends to be olive in tone. They have a distinct Portuguese look.

Since 1975, Portugal has had a large population of people from Angola and some of the other former African colonies. The number is estimated at about 350,000.

women, who had little formal education. Higher education is still rare. The number of children in Portugal who complete at least nine years of school is far lower than in the rest of the European Union. Education is compulsory and free up to age fifteen.

Flood of Refugees

Refugees wait in line for relief goods being handed out.

In 1974, when Portugal's colonial empire ended, a flood of refugees, mainly from Angola, rushed into the country. Portugal had always called its colonial holdings its "overseas territories," and thought of them as part of Portugal. Suddenly, the people of Portugal were faced with an influx of residents from the overseas territories wanting to live in Portugal. The remarkable thing is that Portugal managed to absorb 350,000 people—90 percent of them from Angola—in a very short time. Without enough housing, even for its usual population, the Portuguese government placed refugee families in hotels all over Lisbon, including many of the top hotels in the country.

Others wound up in shantytowns, called *barracas*, where housing was very basic. However, for immigrants who were fleeing for their lives, trying to get away from a brutal civil war, at least this was a safe place where they could begin to put their lives back together. In a short time, the Portuguese found housing for the refugees and people moved out of the hotels. Apartment buildings were erected in suburbs of Lisbon especially for the refugees. The fact that all the refugees spoke Portuguese helped them integrate quickly into daily life. Although the refugees were nearly all black Angolans, there was little resistance to taking in people of another race.

Stable Population

This influx of people should have pushed the total population figure up, but it was balanced by a steady flow of Portuguese leaving the country. It has been a tradition for Portuguese to leave their country to look for work. Back in the 1920s, and for the next forty years, 1.3 million of the 7 million Portuguese left the country. Today, they continue to leave. They go away to find employment because Portugal does not have enough jobs to keep them at home. Many leave because there is a shortage of housing in Portugal. Many of the migrants who leave Portugal are not well educated and take work that requires manual labor. The least-educated people are not likely to speak another language. This keeps them from integrating fully into their host countries and they often live in Portuguese-speaking communities. The single biggest destination is France, where an estimated 750,000 Portuguese

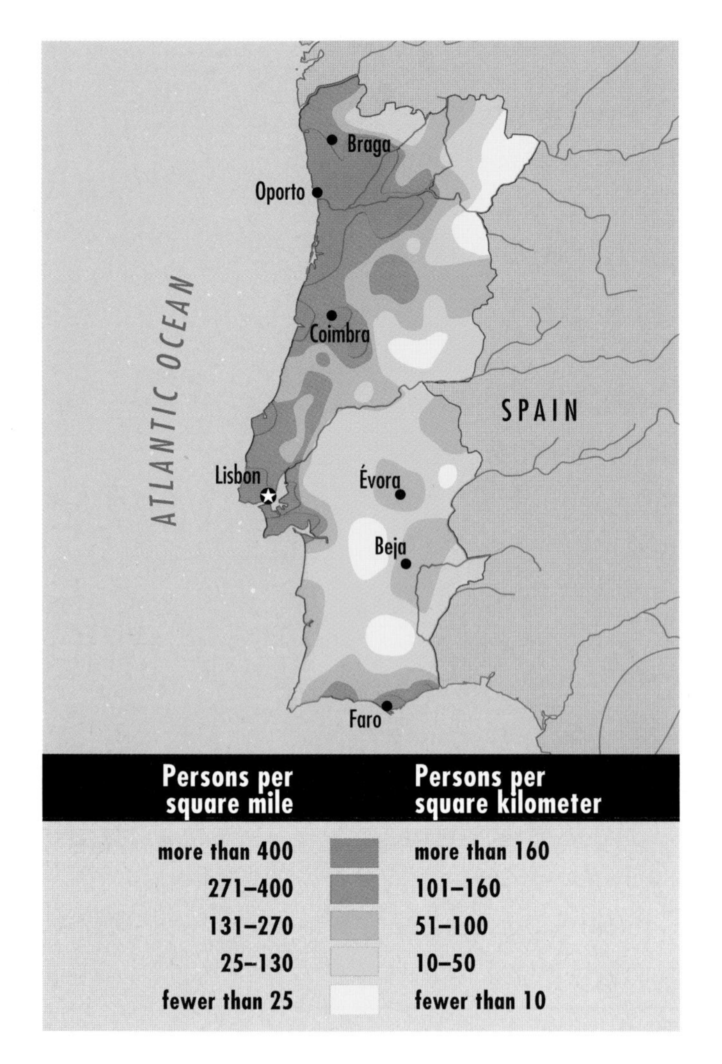

live and work. Paris, the capital of France, has the largest Portuguese population outside Lisbon. Most better-educated Portuguese speak French. Even in the past, when the Portuguese learned a foreign language, they always preferred to learn French, not Spanish. In the 1970s, it was rare to find someone in Lisbon who spoke English. Today, many Portuguese have learned English as well, and it is rare to find someone in Lisbon who doesn't speak at least a little English.

In Portuguese schools, two foreign languages are compulsory. At about the age of ten, students begin one foreign language. It is often English but they may choose French or another European language. After two years, they add a second foreign language. As a result, many Portuguese in their twenties are fluent in two foreign languages.

Where the Portuguese Live (1991)

Lisbon	681,063
Oporto	309,485
Amadora	176,137
Coimbra	147,722
Setubal	103,241

The Universities

The University of Coimbra, founded in 1537, is one of the oldest in Europe. Other major universities are the University of Lisbon, the Technical University of Lisbon, and the

University of Oporto. The University of Evora in the south, founded in 1559, ranks as the second-oldest in Portugal. Evora was a very important city at that time. The school began as a Jesuit institution, but offered the sciences, geography, and mathematics, as well as theology. After this ambitious beginning, the university was forced to close in 1759 when the Jesuits were forced out of Portugal by the Marquês de Pombal.

Exterior view of Coimbra University, Portugal's oldest.

More than 200 years later, in 1973, it was reopened. Today, it has 7,000 undergraduate students and a small postgraduate student body of 200.

The University of Coimbra, in the north, dominates the town of Coimbra. Although the university was founded in 1537, it actually dates back to 1288 when a group of educators were first sponsored by the churches in Lisbon. They even received the blessing of the pope in 1290. The university moved back and forth from Lisbon to Coimbra several times until it settled in Coimbra in 1537. Like the University of Evora, Coimbra was run by the Jesuits. Students may be seen walking through the old streets wearing their distinctive black capes, with colored ribbons attached. They stroll about, often

Graduates of Coimbra University wave to onlookers.

How to Say It

Portuguese is part of the Romance language group that includes French and Spanish, but its pronunciation is very different. The spoken language has a "whooshy" soft quality that makes it more difficult to pronounce than Spanish. Also, certain letters have different pronunciations than we would expect. For example, the letter "s" is usually pronounced "sh" which means a name can sound quite different from its spelling. A typical example is the town of Cascais which is pronounced *kash-kaish*. There is also a nasal sound to some vowels, especially at the ends of words. The word for "no" in Portuguese is spelled não, with a tilde (~) over the a. It sounds more like "now." Many sounds are run together at the ends of words. The symbol "~" combined with "ao" create a nasal sound.

singing Coimbra-style *fados*, the unique music of Portugal. The Coimbra fados are different from those of Lisbon. They are more romantic and not as sad.

Common Portuguese Words and Phrases

Ola	(oh-LAH)	Hello
Boa-tarde	(boh-uh-tard')	Good afternoon
Boa-noite	(boh-uh-noyt')	Good night
Faz favor	(FASH fuh-VOR)	Please
Obrigado	(o-bree-GAH-doo)	Thank you
Desculpte	(dish-KOOLP')	I'm sorry
Quente	(kent')	Hot
Frio	(FREE-ooq)	Cold

A Nation of Catholics

There is a saying in Portugal, "To be Portuguese is to be Catholic" and that accurately describes the importance of the religion in the country today. About 97 percent of the people belong to this religion although not everyone attends church every week. About one-third of the people attend weekly church service but many more observe the religious rituals at the most important times of their lives. A growing number of young people are choosing to marry in a civil ceremony, without a Catholic priest, but nearly all of them have their children baptized. While some may not believe in the rite themselves, they feel they must honor their parents by going through with this ritual. People also often seek out a priest at the end of their lives. At these times, the Portuguese turn to their church for support and for the comfort of rituals.

Opposite: **Parishioners leave the Church of Sao Ildefonso after mass.**

Religion in Portugal

Roman Catholic	97%
Protestant	2%
Other	1%

Many Portuguese attend mass services at least once a week.

National Holidays

Because 99 percent of the country is Christian, Portugal celebrates Christmas as a national holiday. Children look forward to the arrival of "Father Christmas," who leaves presents under the Christmas tree or in shoes left by the fireplace. The traditional dinner is bacalhau, a dish of salt cod and boiled potatoes.

Holiday Celebrations

The Three Wise Men	January
Mardi Gras	February/March
Liberty Day	April 25
Our Lady of Fátima	May 13
Feast of Corpus Christi	June 6
Day of Camões	June 10
Feast of St. Anthony (Lisbon)	June 13
Feast of the Assumption	August 8
Proclamation of the Republic	October 5
All Saints' Day	November 1
Restoration of Independence	December 1
Feast of the Immaculate Conception	December 8
Christmas	December 25

In spite of the close identification of the Portuguese people with the Roman Catholic Church, the government and the religions are kept strictly apart. This principle, similar to that of the United States, has been part of the country's laws since the First Republic began in 1910 and it was also made part of the constitution of 1976. However, in practice, many parts of everyday life are connected to the moral laws of the church.

Freedom of Worship

When Portugal went through its peaceful revolution in 1974, the role and power of the Catholic Church returned to a more normal position. The new constitution specifically guarantees the right of all people to practice their faith, no matter what

Manueline Architecture

Jeronimos Monastery (pictured) was built to honor Vasco da Gama's journey to India in 1497 and his successful return. It is one of many buildings in the Manueline style, named for King Manuel. He chose the site for the monastery at Belém, where a chapel was originally founded by Prince Henry the Navigator. The Manueline style is the Portuguese name for Gothic architecture, which features ornate carving and elaborate decoration. It may be seen on monasteries in Coimbra and Evora and on the National Palace in Sintra. Jeronimos is a massive building. Even though it is covered with detailed ornamentation, it was built so well that it survived the terrible earthquake of 1755, which virtually leveled the city of Lisbon.

Fátima

On May 13, 1917, in the center of Portugal, three children (pictured) in the village of Fátima reported seeing a vision of the Virgin Mary. Each month after that, also on the thirteenth day, the vision returned. Crowds numbering in the tens of thousands gathered to see this vision. The tiny city has since become a place of pilgrimage. Pope Paul VI came to Fátima on May 13, 1967, to mark the fiftieth anniversary of the first vision. On May 13, 2000, Pope John Paul II traveled to Fátima where he blessed two of the children, Jacinta Marto and her brother Francisco, in a ritual called beatification. The children said that Mary told them three secrets. According to the legend, the secrets were predictions about the end of the first World War and the period of Communism that would follow. The third secret, revealed during Pope John Paul II's appearance, said that someone would attempt to kill a pope. The attack on John Paul II's life in 1981 inspired his visit to Fátima in 2000.

religion they follow. People were free to worship as they saw fit but the Church no longer had control over their lives. The constitution created the formal separation, and the changing way of life in Portugal made this separation a reality. In practice, however, very few Jews came to live in Portugal; it is estimated that by the 1990s, there were no more than 1,000 Jews in Portugal, most of them in Lisbon. Islam returned to Portugal with the flood of immigrants from the former colonies in southern Africa as well as immigrant workers coming across the sea from Morocco.

Although church buildings still occupy prominent places in Portugal, often sitting on hillsides that look out over the village itself, religious practice has declined. At the same time, there is often not enough money needed to preserve these beautiful buildings and they are sometimes run-down and in need of repair. At the height of Salazar's rule, it was considered a great honor for one of the sons in a family to enter the priesthood. Today, few Portuguese men consider this a desirable occupation.

Cardinals Named

In February 2001, Pope John Paul II named forty-four new cardinals from twenty-seven countries. Among them were two Portuguese, Dom José Policarpo and Dom José Saraiva Martins. The consecration ceremony took place in St. Peter's Square in Rome. The appointments were a reflection of Portugal's position as a country where nearly all the people follow the Roman Catholic religion.

Leisure Time the Portuguese Way

Opposite: **Relaxing at the Botanical Gardens café.**

THE WIDEST VARIETY OF CULTURAL ACTIVITIES CAN BE found in Portugal, especially in the cities. In spite of its small size, the country has nurtured a unique musical tradition as well as a strong literary tradition. Many people are devoted to soccer and follow the successes and failures of the national teams very closely. Many others enjoy Lisbon's great museums as well as the small ones that are devoted to one subject. Most of the people strolling through the city's museums are Portuguese. They spend their leisure time enjoying Portuguese art, sculpture, tile work, and all the work shown in more than two dozen museums. They visit the city's botanical gardens, the beaches in the seaside town of Cascais, or make a pilgrimage to the religious shrine at Fátima. There are often foreign ships docked in Lisbon where visitors are welcome. Exploring the deck of a great sailing ship is fun for the entire family. They take their time sitting at sidewalk cafes around the Rossio in Lisbon, where the parents enjoy pastries with coffee and the children have soft drinks.

Beach Towns

An electric train from Lisbon takes people to the seaside resorts of Estoril and Cascais in less than an hour. It's a pleasant way to spend a day. These towns are rich in history but also offer a pleasant day at the beach. Estoril was once known as the town where the deposed kings of Europe lived quietly

Sunbathers enjoying a beautiful Algarve beach.

but luxuriously while they waited to see if they would ever be kings again. Cascais was a small fishing village that has exploded in size and is no longer a sleepy little beach town. Fishing is still an important activity but visitors can now find oceanfront restaurants and a variety of modern shops.

The Algarve is one of the most-visited parts of the country. Its beautiful beaches are clean and inviting and the region is known for its many sunny days. Charming towns filled with souvenir shops selling traditional Portuguese products as well as excellent food and friendly people have made the Algarve a popular destination, especially for other Europeans.

Azulejos

Azulejos is the Portuguese word for ceramic tiles. The word actually means "blue." Some people think the word is used for the tiles because many of the earliest ones were blue.

One hundred and seventy tiles make up this mural on a city building.

National Palace

Sintra, a hilltop town just 20 miles (32 km) from Lisbon, has traditionally been the summer home of Portuguese royalty and is now so crowded with tourists that its narrow streets are filled to capacity. The National Palace in Sintra is just one of many intriguing buildings that make the town such a fascinating destination. This building, dating from the fourteenth and fifteenth centuries, allows visitors a look at the way life was lived here more than 500 years ago. Tour guides describe the way the staff served the royal families who lived there. The National Palace hosted some of the most important Portuguese writers and artists in history and continues to be a beautiful setting for concerts and official receptions.

However, the word comes from the Arabic word *azraq* and arrived in Portugal along with the tiles themselves, when the Muslim Moors invaded the Iberian Peninsula. The tiles may be worked right into the wall of a building, either inside or out, like a mural. A tile is a piece of ceramic clay that has been painted and then baked in an oven. This makes the design last a very long time. Most of these early tiles showed only geometric patterns because Islam does not permit images of any living things to be used When the Portuguese began to make tiles in Lisbon in the sixteenth century, blue and yellow were the most popular colors. Portuguese tiles can be seen almost everywhere in Lisbon, but the place that is devoted to them is the tile museum, which is located in an old convent. Here you can see a mural that shows what Lisbon looked like before the earthquake of 1755. This tile mural actually survived the earthquake! Modern tile murals may be found in some subway

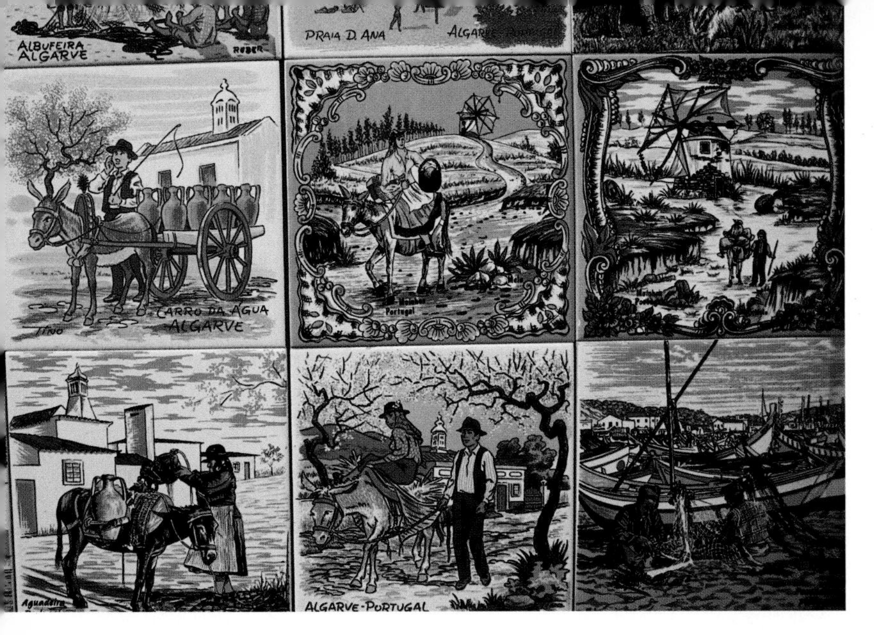

Portuguese culture is shown on tiles found in the Algarve region.

stations, including the new station built for Expo '98, the Portuguese World's Fair. One of the most spectacular examples is at the São Bento train station in the city of Oporto. These huge tile murals portray scenes from Portuguese history.

Fado

Fado is a Portuguese word meaning "fate" or "destiny." It is also the name of a form of music that began in Lisbon in the

Luís de Camões

Although he lived 500 years ago, Luís de Camões (1523–1580) is still considered Portugal's greatest poet. He is often called a soldier-poet because he followed both callings at the same time. He was imprisoned and banished to the tiny colony of Goa in India in 1553. His work, *Os Lusiadas* ("The Lusitanians"), was published in 1572. In it, Camões used the voyages of Vasco da Gama to talk about the Portuguese people. It is still considered the ultimate example of Portuguese writing even though Portugal has always had important writers, including Nobel medalist José Saramago. Politicians in Portugal have made great use of quotes taken from *Os Lusiadas* just as those in the United States refer to the Gettysburg Address of Abraham Lincoln or Martin Luther King, Jr.'s "I Have A Dream" speech. *Os Lusiadas* is written in a romantic style, full of exciting images describing Portugal's history up to that time. Today, the Camões Institute and the Camões Center continue in his spirit, emphasizing Portuguese culture. The institute sends teachers and scholars around the world to share Portuguese language and culture.

Amália Rodrigues

The most famous fado singer was Amália Rodrigues (1925–1999). Many fados were written specifically for her. Her rich voice and dramatic style of singing seemed to sum up everything about the fado. She recorded many albums and also played to audiences around the world. Even when people could not understand the words she sang, because they did not speak Portuguese, they could feel the emotion in her voice and they could relate to the mood she portrayed.

early nineteenth century. Fado expresses the character of the Portuguese people, a sense that fate determines everyday life. The Portuguese guitar, a beautiful instrument with a rounded body, was introduced in the eighteenth century, first in Oporto. Around 1870, guitars began to accompany the fado singer, who is often a woman and who is known as a *fadista*, a fado singer. The music was so popular that King Don Carlos learned to play the guitar in order to play fado music. Fado was considered the music of city and urban life but it became very popular in the 1920s and 1930s when it was played on the radio. The creation of the National Radio Broadcasting network in 1935 helped spread the sound even farther. But it was only in 1957, when Portuguese television was first broadcast, that the faces of the artists became known.

But fado is not just music of the past. A young singer called Misia is known as "the new

Misia performs with U.S. dancer and choreographer Bill T. Jones.

Fado Museum

A new museum opened in 1999 dedicated to the fado. It is called the Fado Museum, and it is situated in the Alfama section of Lisbon, where fado took root. Although all of Lisbon is very historic, the Alfama is one of the oldest parts of the city. Some of the buildings date back to the twelfth century. In the museum, the history of the fado is shown through photographs, musical instruments, and in little scenes. As the visitor walks through, bits of music are played. There is even a room set up as a typical tavern where people would go to hear fado. Figures of the fado singer and the musicians are on a stage, with tables and chairs for the visitors. As you sit down, the lights are dimmed, the music begins, and the fadista sings her song. For the real thing, of course, anyone can visit a nightclub where fado is still performed.

queen of fado." She was born in Oporto and combines this old form of music with very modern ideas. Her dramatic stage performances have already brought her great acceptance in Europe. Misia works with contemporary composers and writers to record her music. She emphasizes the idea of the fado as

Calouste Gulbenkian

One of the best-known people in Portugal wasn't even Portuguese. Calouste Gulbenkian was a wealthy Armenian oil businessman who took refuge in Portugal during World War II. He was so grateful to his adopted country that he left his entire estate to the Portuguese to be used to develop cultural institutions. The Gulbenkian Museum is filled with art that he collected during his lifetime. He seemed to love everything because he collected Chinese porcelain, paintings, sculpture, Egyptian art, Islamic art, and European paintings. The museum is set in a beautiful park. As visitors walk through the museum, its many large windows bring the park into view. Gulbenkian's estate is also used to fund study in several areas of art. His scholarships have permitted many young people to study in their chosen fields.

National Museum of Ancient Art

Museu Nacional de Arte Antiga (National Museum of Ancient Art) is home to Portugal's national art collection. It is located in a beautiful sixteenth-century building that was once a palace. The museum itself opened in 1884. In addition to the largest collection of paintings in Portugal, it has many other treasures. Among the many collections are Japanese screens; Portuguese and Chinese ceramics; silver, gold, and jewelry; tapestries, textiles, and furniture. The museum also features a collection of ivory and furniture from Portugal's Asian and African possessions. It is also known for its large collection of religious paintings from different periods of history. One of the many highlights of the museum's painting collection, which covers a period of 500 years, is *The Temptations of St. Anthony* by Hieronymus Bosch.

the music of the cities. She has already received awards for her work and is having as great an impact on the present generation as Amália had on hers.

A view of the Expo '98 fair grounds.

Park of the Nations

In 1998, Lisbon hosted a spectacular world's fair—Expo '98. When the fair closed, the huge site, stretching for 3 miles (5 km) along the Tagus River, was converted into a great park for the people. The major exhibits had been designed with this purpose in mind, so the Park of the Nations is now a major entertainment complex. One of the main attractions is a fascinating aquarium that contains fish from all the oceans of the world. Visitors walk through the aquarium with water all around them. To be sure the park was easy to get to, a new metro (subway) station was opened right at the entrance. Its walls are covered with murals depicting water themes, and made of tiles, a typical Portuguese touch.

Portuguese Children's Games

Many games in Portugal are just like those played by children in the United States. There are playground games with jump ropes, chalk, and tops. A game that seems to be an original with Portuguese children is *O senhor barqueiro*, which means "The Ferryman."

To begin this game, two children hold hands to form an arch. They think of the name of something such as a fruit, an animal, or a country, without letting the other children know what they are thinking of.

The other children line up in a row and sing a song, "Oh, Ferryman, please let me pass. I have two little children which I can no longer provide for. I shall pass, I shall pass . . . but someone will be left behind, if not the mother in the front, then the children in the back."

All the children pass under the arch until the last one in the row is trapped inside the arch. The two children forming the arch then say a list of names for the child who is trapped. That child must choose one. Depending on the answer the trapped child gives, he or she then stands behind one of the two children forming the arch.

This goes on until every child has been trapped and has made a choice of one of the names. The result is two rows of children who now form two teams. The two teams stand on opposite sides of a line drawn on the ground. The children in front hold arms and then all the other children pull, in a tug-of-war, trying to pull the opposing player onto their side of the line.

When all the children have been pulled over to one side, that side wins.

Portugal's early explorers are carved into the Monument to the Discoverers.

Monument to the Discoverers

The Monument to the Discoverers, built in 1960, is a huge sculpture that presents the human side of the people it celebrates. The monument, which was built on the shore of the Tagus River, is in the form of a caravel, the sailing ship used by the early explorers. The important figures of the explorations are carved into the prow, looking out to sea. At the front is Prince Henry the Navigator who inspired their journeys. While you can visit the monument from the shore, it is best seen from a sightseeing boat on the river. That way, you can see how the entire sculpture juts out over the water, as if it were going to take off on a journey of its own.

Soccer

Many Portuguese men and boys devote their spare time to soccer. Soccer news is eagerly read and the progress of the Portuguese teams is closely followed. Portugal's national team, Benfica, is highly rated. Portugal usually ranks fourth in the world and is a strong contender in World Cup competitions. The matches that take place all over Europe every week have fans glued to their television sets when they can't attend in person. Soccer really consumes sports fans in Europe. It's as if all of America's baseball, football, and basketball stars were in the same sport and all the fans were following that one sport. Soccer is played throughout Africa, Latin America, and Europe.

The national soccer team, Benfica (left), has a large following in Portugal.

Eusebio

Although Portugal's soccer team is currently doing very well, its most famous soccer player was a star of the 1960s, known by just one name—Eusebio. This brilliant player, whose full name is Eusebio da Silva Ferreira, was born in Mozambique, a colony of Portugal. He came to play for Portugal in 1958 and was the star of the Benfica team from 1961 until he retired in 1975. He was top scorer in the 1966 World Cup, with nine goals. Eusebio was known as "The Black Panther" and "The Black Pearl." He was a member of a dozen Portuguese championship teams.

Bullfighting

The sport of bullfighting, called the *tourada* in Portugal, takes place during a season that usually starts on Easter Sunday and ends in October, much like the baseball season in the United States. Since it takes place outdoors, the weather must be pleasant.

Bullfights are usually staged twice a week, on Thursdays and Sundays, and go on for several hours. The fight itself is actually in three parts, with different men playing their own roles. These three groups are the *cavaleiros*, the *toureiros*, and the *forcados*. The contest begins with the cavaleiro mounted on a horse. The horse, guided by the cavaleiro, dances around the bull, which charges at this confusing target over and over again, until it is tired out. The crowd applauds and cheers when the cavaleiro does something graceful and dangerous. The toureiros are on the ground with the bull. They run around with bright yellow and pink capes, and try to make the bull angry so that it will charge. Finally, the forcados, armed only with a wooden fork, charge right at the bull and try to wrestle it to the ground with their bare hands. The bull may weigh as much as half a ton (1,000 pounds). At this point, the bull is exhausted and can be led from the ring.

Bullfighting is a controversial sport wherever it takes place. Many people believe that it is an uneven fight, not really a fight at all, since the bull is clearly going to lose his life at the end of it. In Spain and Mexico, at the end of the fight, the bullfighter thrusts his sword into the bull and kills it right in front of the crowd. Portugal puts a slightly different twist to it. The bull is still alive when it leaves the arena, but not for long. As soon as it leaves the ring, it is slaughtered. The bull has certainly suffered during its time in the ring where darts are thrust into it by the cavaleiro. Most Portuguese enjoy the horsemanship and the bright costumes.

In addition to soccer, Portugal's runners have taken the world stage on many occasions. Rosa Mota has won the women's Boston Marathon three times, in 1987, 1988, and 1990. Portuguese athletes won two bronze medals in the 2000 Olympics: Nuno Delgado won a bronze medal in the men's Judo 178-pound (81-kg) division and Fernanda Ribeiro won a bronze in the women's 10,000-meter track event.

Rosa Mota leads at the London Marathon in 1992.

Nobel Prize Winners

In 1949, the Nobel Prize in medicine was shared by two men—Walter Rudolf Hess, a Swiss scientist, and Antõnio Caetano de Abreu Freire Egas Moniz, a Portuguese scientist. Dr. Moniz's work was widely published during his long career and he taught at Coimbra University. Only the most significant work in each field is honored by the Nobel committee, which meets each year in Sweden to announce these awards. They are often given for a lifetime of work.

That was true of José Saramago, the 1998 winner of the Nobel Prize in Literature. This Portuguese author was honored for his novels, mysterious and complicated stories that show a brilliant mind at work. Some of his works include *Blindness*, *The Tale of the Unknown Island*, and *All the Names*. Each of these works has found an international audience through translation. He presents intriguing ideas to the reader. In *The History of the Siege of Lisbon*, he shows what might happen when an editor changes one word in a history book and tries to rewrite history.

José Saramago shows his medal after receiving the Nobel Prize in literature.

CHAPTER TEN

A Unique Way of Life

In spite of the many changes taking place in Portugal, the Portuguese people still combine a reserved manner with genuine friendliness and warmth. Most Portuguese would not approach you first, but if you strike up a conversation, they are delighted and eager to share their country with you. Their reserved manner is considered an expression of the quality known as *saudade* which translates loosely to "longing," a feeling of sadness mixed with hope. Even though the borders that separate the countries of Europe are becoming easier to cross, you would never confuse a Portuguese person with a French person or with a Spanish person who lives in the neighboring country. This national personality is one of the elements that makes Portugal a fascinating place to visit.

Opposite: **An improved economy has changed life for many Portuguese.**

The Portuguese are known to be warm and friendly people.

The kind of life a Portuguese person lives depends very much on whether that person is born in the city or in the countryside. Farmers' days are filled with hard work. Many still use very basic equipment such as wooden plows, and rely on their own hard labor. Their way of life is little changed from the past. The farther north you travel, the fewer changes you will see. But in the cities, and in the south, change has come very quickly. In the years after the 1974 revolution, and especially since Portugal became a member of the European Community, change has been as dramatic as at any time in history. The European Community has pushed Portugal to improve its economy, and has poured a great deal of money into the effort to modernize the nation.

Social Structure

During the long period of the Salazar dictatorship, Portugal scarcely changed at all. In many ways, it remained the most "European" of the nations that make up Europe. The buildings were reminders of the past, and the people seemed to be living in the past too. People lived according to the class they were born into, whether they came from the lower class or the upper class. There were not very many people in the middle class. Social standing was difficult to overcome during the long decades of the dictatorship. Change began slowly as the economy began to develop in the 1960s. With the growth of a middle class, it became easier for people to improve their social status.

The move to join the European Union (EU) brought about even more change. Portugal was called "the poor man of Europe," and had a long way to go to catch up with its more productive neighbors. The EU poured money into Portugal and changes began, although the essential nature of the Portuguese people has not changed. While the shops are now full of trendy clothing and electronic gear, and the Internet is part of daily life, the Portuguese people continue to treasure their family life and maintain their festivals and traditions.

A Year of Festivals

Throughout Portugal, from north to south, and on the islands of Madeira and the Azores, festivals, fairs, and other events highlight the calendar. Religious observances are at the heart of many festivals, especially those that take place during Easter. In Barcelos, the Festival of the Crosses celebrates the day a cross appeared on earth in 1504. In the Azores, the Senhor Santo Cristo Festival includes a magnificent procession, the most elaborate in all of Portugal. Millions of lights, flags, and flowers are used to decorate the entire town for the festival, which lasts for several

The Church of Esperanca lit up for the Senhor Santo Cristo Festival.

days. It is a joyous celebration but also one with very serious religious rituals.

In Oporto, the Festival of São João is held on June 24. Appropriately for a port city and fishing town, the festival includes a boat race. In Lisbon, the Festival of Saint Anthony, on June 12 or 13, includes parades and floats on the main street, called Avenida da Liberdade. The singers and dancers make their way up into the Alfama district of the city. The Festival of Sintra is a cultural event that takes place in July. It features recitals, concerts, and ballet performances at the National Palace and the Queluz Palace.

The Rose Festival is celebrated in Vila Franco do Lima.

A different kind of festival takes place in Coimbra at the end of the university year in May. Graduating students celebrate the *Queima das Fitas*, the "Burning of the Ribbons." These are the symbols of each student's studies. Each school specializes in a different subject such as medicine and each has its own colored ribbon.

Celebrations at the end of a successful harvest in Moita and other regions are tied to the country's agricultural roots.

In August, a national folklore festival is held in the Algarve followed by a song and dance festival in September. Our Lady of Fátima, a year-round site for celebration, is the focus of special pilgrimages in May and October.

National Dish

More than one delicious food can be called the national dish of Portugal, but many would say it is anything made with bacalhau—dried and salted codfish. The Portuguese use bacalhau in regional specialties such as *pasteis de balcalhau*, or fried fish cakes, and *bacalhau a Gomes de Sa*, a dish made with salt cod, potatoes, onions, olives, and hard-boiled eggs. Others would claim the honor of national dish for *sardinhas assadas*, or simple grilled sardines. Portuguese sardines are very large and a few of them with a vegetable make a hearty meal. Two Portuguese elements come together in *porco a alentejana*, a dish that combines pork and clams. The dish is usually cooked in a *cataplana*, a covered pot that keeps the food moist while it is cooking. Portugal's best-known soup, is *caldo verde*, which is made from a green vegetable similar to kale. Caldo verde is made in Portugal's luxury hotels and its country homes.

A Recipe for *Bacalhau*

Ingredients:

2 pounds salt cod, soaked in water
2 large onions, sliced thin
1/3 cup butter
1 clove garlic, minced
2 tablespoons bread crumbs
9 small red potatoes
1 teaspoon salt
10 medium green olives, pitted
10 medium black olives, pitted
3 large eggs, hard-boiled, peeled and sliced
2 tablespoons vinegar
2 tablespoons olive oil
1/2 teaspoon black pepper, freshly ground

Method:

1. Soak dried salt cod overnight in water. Change the water at least twice. Drain before cooking.
2. Place cod in a pan. Cover with clear water. Bring to a boil, then simmer on low heat for 15 minutes.
3. In a separate pan, boil the potatoes in water with 1 teaspoon salt. Cook about 20–25 minutes. Drain water, cut potatoes into 4 to 6 wedges.
4. Drain the liquid. Remove bones and skin from the fish. Cut fish into spoon-sized pieces.
5. In a frying pan, sauté sliced onions in half the butter. Add the garlic, and continue cooking until golden brown.
6. With remaining butter, grease the bottom and sides of a 2-quart casserole dish. Heat oven to 350°F.
7. Layer half each of onions, potatoes, and cod in the dish. Sprinkle with pepper, then repeat the layering. Sprinkle with bread crumbs. Bake for 15 minutes.
8. To serve, sprinkle with olives and egg slices. Mix vinegar and olive oil in a small bowl. Drizzle over the fish. Serves 4.

Camões Day

June 10 is known as Camões Day and also Portuguese National Day as well as *Dia de Portugal e das Communidades*. The Portuguese title refers to Portuguese communities around the world that mark this important occasion. One of the largest celebrations takes place in Newark, New Jersey, which has a large Portuguese community. In Lisbon, people come to the statue of Camões in Praca Luis de Camões, the square honoring Portugal's national poet. Camões is best known for his epic poem called *Os Lusiadas* (the Portuguese), which describes the explorers' travels around the world.

City Life

Strolling around the streets of Lisbon, Portugal's capital city, is like taking a trip back in time. It is also a way to see how people in Portugal live today. The houses are jammed together on small streets in neighborhoods built on Lisbon's seven hills. Tiny shops often occupy the first floor of these buildings, with a small restaurant or grocery store crammed with food or other goods. The family may live upstairs, above the shop. These little family businesses take care of the needs of the neighborhood. There are no supermarkets in the older neighborhoods. The sidewalks are barely wide enough for one person to walk by and if two people are walking toward one another, one of them must step into the street to let the other person go by. There's no need to push ahead, it's just polite to let someone walk by. Cars travel the main streets of the Bairro Alto, Alfama, and Castelo, three of the oldest districts, but they do so on one-way streets. Many of the tinier streets are wide enough for only carts and pedestrians.

Brightly colored urban homes in Oporto

Modern malls are similar to those in the United States.

Shopping Malls

The biggest changes taking place in Portugal today may be seen in the new malls and shopping centers. Traditional Portuguese life revolved around small cafés, scarcely big enough for five or six tables, where neighborhood people came to talk and enjoy a small cup of strong coffee. The new malls have a Portuguese flavor but they are patterned after the big, busy shopping centers of the United States. In Lisbon, the arrival of Amoreiras, a glittering, modern urban shopping mall complete with video stores, cinemas, fast-food restaurants, and hundreds of shops, had the impact of a space ship landing in a downtown area.

Although families come to the mall, teenagers enjoy hanging out in Amoreiras to meet their friends. It is the sight of young people out on their own, or in groups of friends, that shows some of the biggest social differences in Portugal since the country became part of the European Union. No one lingers long over a meal here. The idea is to eat, then move on and shop some more. Amoreiras is part of an even larger complex that includes a huge office building, hotels, and apartments. The look of the architecture is closer to Disneyland than to the traditional stone buildings of Lisbon.

Malling the Algarve

A similar mall is now planned for southern Portugal, where it is likely to have an even bigger impact. With more than 100 stores, Forum Algarve, the mall in the town of Faro, has many local shop owners worried. They're afraid that the new mall, which also has twenty restaurants and nine cinemas, will take all the business away from them. The mall will also change the character of the region, which is a major tourist destination. Although tourists come for the local flavor, they will probably flock to the mall, which will have many foreign shops. Only 15 percent of the mall's shops are owned by local firms. The scale of the project is huge for this small area. The builders expect to see 800,000 visitors each month, which will put a heavy strain on the environment. This kind of growth is a problem for Portugal, which is trying to expand its economy without destroying the special attractions that make it such an interesting place to visit.

As one of the countries of the European Union, Portugal today is undergoing the biggest changes since the Revolution of the Carnations. Its way of life must fit into the greater European community and yet it must find a way to preserve its traditions, the things that make Portugal a unique culture and nation.

Timeline

Portuguese History

Phoenicians settle in present-day Portugal.	1000s B.C
Portugal becomes part of the Roman Empire.	100s B.C
Muslim Moors from North Africa invade Spain and Portugal.	A.D. 711
Portugal gains its independence.	1143
Da Gama sets sail for India.	1497

World History

2500 B.C.	Egyptians build the Pyramids and the Sphinx in Giza.
563 B.C.	The Buddha is born in India.
A.D. 313	The Roman emperor Constantine recognizes Christianity.
610	The Prophet Muhammad begins preaching a new religion called Islam.
1054	The Eastern (Orthodox) and Western (Roman) Churches break apart.
1066	William the Conqueror defeats the English in the Battle of Hastings.
1095	Pope Urban II proclaims the First Crusade.
1215	King John seals the Magna Carta.
1300s	The Renaissance begins in Italy.
1347	The Black Death sweeps through Europe.
1453	Ottoman Turks capture Constantinople, conquering the Byzantine Empire.
1492	Columbus arrives in North America.

Portuguese History

Cabral claims Brazil for Portugal.	1500
Spain conquers Portugal.	1580
Portugal regains its independence from Spain.	1640
Portugal becomes a republic.	1910
António Salazar takes over as dictator.	1928
A revolution in Portugal ousts dictatorial rule.	1974
A new Constitution allows women to vote, free elections held.	1976
Portugal joins the European Community.	1986
Portugal serves as leader of the European Community program.	2000

World History

1500s	The Reformation leads to the birth of Protestantism.
1776	The Declaration of Independence is signed.
1789	The French Revolution begins.
1865	The American Civil War ends.
1914	World War I breaks out.
1917	The Bolshevik Revolution brings communism to Russia.
1929	Worldwide economic depression begins.
1939	World War II begins, following the German invasion of Poland.
1945	World War II ends.
1957	The Vietnam War starts.
1969	Humans land on the moon.
1975	The Vietnam War ends.
1979	Soviet Union invades Afghanistan.
1983	Drought and famine in Africa.
1989	The Berlin Wall is torn down, as communism crumbles in Eastern Europe.
1991	Soviet Union breaks into separate states.
1992	Bill Clinton is elected U.S. president.
2000	George W. Bush is elected U.S. president.

Fast Facts

Official name:	Republic of Portugal
Capital:	Lisbon
Official language:	Portuguese

Oporto

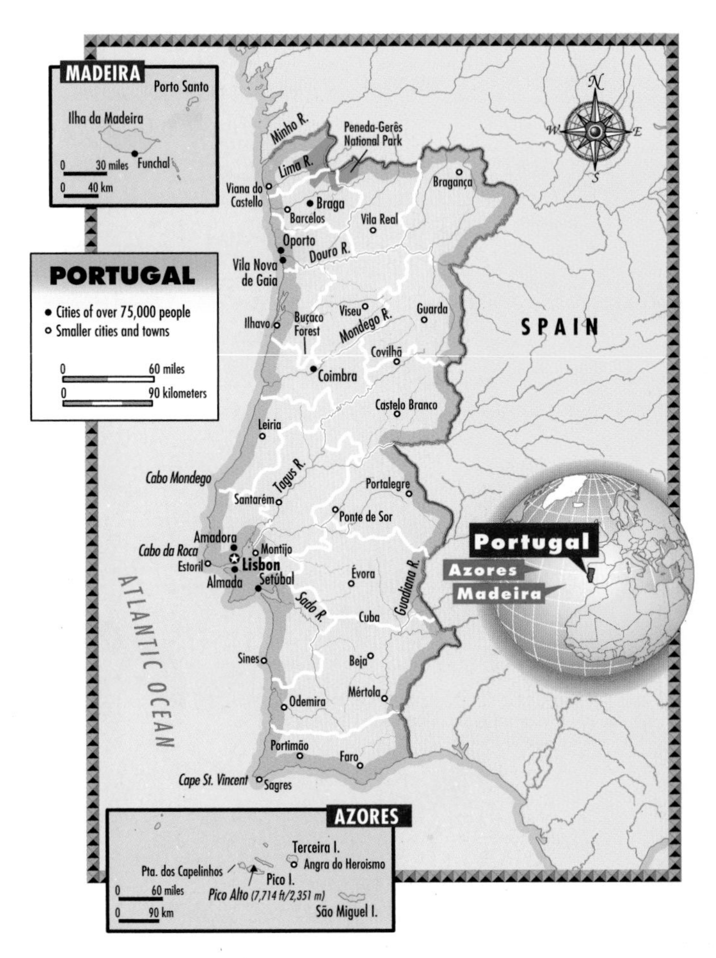

Portugal's flag

Cabo da Roca

Religions:	97% Roman Catholic; 2% Protestant; 1% other
Founding date:	1143
National anthem:	*Á Portuguesa* ("The Portuguese")
Overseas provinces:	Madeira, Azores
Government:	Republic with one legislative house
Chief of state:	President
Head of government:	Prime Minister
Legislature:	Assembly of the Republic, 230 members
Administrative divisions:	18 districts, 2 autonomous regions
Area:	35,550 square miles (92,080 sq km)
Highest elevation:	Estrela in Serra da Estrela at 6,539 feet (1,993 m) above sea level
Lowest elevation:	Sea level along the Atlantic Ocean
Longest river:	Tagus (Tejo), 626 miles (1,000 km) (including Spain)
Major rivers:	Douro, Mondego, Tagus, Guadiana, Sado
Major harbors:	Lisbon, Oporto, Leixões, Aveiro, Funchal, Ponta Delgada
Average annual rainfall:	40–51 inches (100–130 cm), north; rainfall, south: 16–24 inches (60 cm)
Average temperatures:	Summer: 68° to 75°F (20° to 24°C); Winter: 48° to 54°F (9° to 12°C)

King Alfonso Henriques

Currency

National population (2000 est.): 10,048,232

Population density: 281 people per square mile (108/sq km)

Distribution: 36% urban, 64% rural

Population of largest cities:

Lisbon	681,063
Oporto	309,485
Amadora	176,137
Coimbra	147,722
Setubal	103,241

Famous landmarks:

- ***Castelo de São Jorge***, Lisbon
- ***Fátima***
- ***Parque Nacional da Serra da Estrela***
- ***Museu Nacional de Arte Antiga***
- ***Belém Tower***
- ***Palácio Nacional de Sintra***
- ***Solar do Vinho do Porto***, Oporto

Industry: Manufacturing: extiles, wood pulp, paper, footwear, cork, wine, ceramics, automotive. Agriculture: grains, potatoes, olives, grapes for wine, livestock. Natural resources: fish, forests, cork, tungsten, iron ore

Currency: Portugal's monetary unit is the euro.
One euro equals 100 cents. 1.14 euros = U.S.$1.

Weights and measures: Metric system

Literacy: 89.6 percent

Friendly faces of Portugal

Luís de Camões

Common Portuguese words and terms:

Ola (oh-LAH)	Hello
Boa-tarde (boh-uh-tard')	Good afternoon
Boa-noite (boh-uh-noyt')	Good night
Faz favor (FASH fuh-VOR)	Please
Obrigado (o-bree-GAH-doo)	Thank you
Desculpte (dish-KOOLP')	I'm sorry
Quente (kent')	Hot
Frio (FREE-ooq)	Cold

Famous Portuguese:

Alfonso I (1110–1185)
Earliest king of Portugal. Born in Guimarãs.

Luís de Camões (1524–1580)
Portugal's greatest poet.

Bartolomeu Dias (1450–1500)
Navigator and explorer. First to sail around the Cape of Good Hope.

Eusebio (1942–)
Soccer star.

Vasco da Gama (1469?–1524)
Navigator and explorer who found a route to India. Founded Natal, Africa.

Henry the Navigator (1394–1460)
Established a school of navigation in Sagres. Was responsible for Portugal's Age of Exploration.

Manuel I (1469–1521)
King of Portugal. Born in Alcochete.

Anibal Cavaco Silva (1939–)
Politician and prime minister from 1985-1995. Born in Loulé.

To Find Out More

Books

- De Skalon, Anna. *We Live in Portugal*. New York: Franklin Watts, 1987.
- Fritz, Jean. *Around the World in a Hundred Years, From Henry the Navigator to Magellan*. New York: Putnam, 1994.
- Geography Department Staff. *Portugal in Pictures*. Minneapolis: Lerner, 1995.
- Moore, Richard. *Portugal*. Austin, TX: Raintree-Steck Vaughn, 1992.

Web Sites

- **Front Page Online**
  www.the-news.net
  This is a weekly Portuguese newspaper, in English, covering a variety of news stories. It includes the main regions of Portugal as well as business and sports news.
- **Welcome to Portugal**
  www.portugal.org
  Full range of subjects and photographs showing Portugal.
- **Portugal Roots Web**
  http://webhome.idirect.com/~geoles
  Portugal Roots Web site with extensive cultural information including music and architecture.

Organizations and Embassies

- **Embassy of Portugal**
  2125 Kalorama Road N.W.
  Washington, DC 20008
  (202) 328-8610

- **Portuguese National Tourist Office**
  590 Fifth Avenue
  New York, NY 10020
  (212) 354-4403

Index

Page numbers in *italics* indicate illustrations.

A

Aeminium. *See* Coimbra.
"Age of the Discoveries," 10
agriculture, 32, 37, 41, 52–53, 62, *74*, 77, 82–84, *82*, 122
 climate and, 27, 32
 cork, 19, 33, *33*, 34, *34*, 84, 85–87, *85*
 olives, 83, *83*
 two-tier cultivation, 36
 winemaking, 26, *26*, 36, 84–85, 88, *88*
Alentejo region, 17, 20, 21, *33*
Alfonso I (king), 45, 49, 133
Alfonso V (king), 53
Alfonso VI (king), 44
Algarve Coast, *14*
Algarve region, 17, 20–21, *20*, 32, 35, 108, *108*
almond trees, 35, *35*
Alqueva Dam, 37–38
Amoreiras, 126–127
Angra do Heroísmo, 22
animal life
 golden eagle, 38, *38*
 Iberian lynx, 38
 Lusitano horses, 38–39, *39*
 Portuguese water dog, 39, *39*
architecture, 25, 42, 103, *103*, 127
 Moors and, 21
 Roman occupation and, *40*, 42–43
Armed Forces movement, 64
Arrábida Bridge, 25
art, 112
Assembly of the Republic, 70
astrolabe, 9–10, *9*, 46, *46*
Azores Islands, 15, 18, 21–22, 46, 50, 52, 70, 73
Azulejos (ceramic tiles), 89, 108–110, *108*, *110*

B

bacalhau (national dish), 76, 123
barco rabelo (wooden boats), 80–82, *80*, *81*
barracas (shantytowns), 95
beatification ritual, 104
Beira region, 17
Benfica soccer team, 115, *115*
Blessing of the Fleet, 79
boat building industry, 80–81
boat racing, 81–82, *81*
bordados (embroidery), 85, *85*
borders, 15, 16, 26
Botanical Gardens, 34, *106*
bougainvillea (plant life), 31, *31*
Brazil colony, 47, 55–56, *55*, 58
Bronze Age, 41
bullfighting, 116, *116*
"Burning of the Ribbons" celebration, 122

C

Cabo da Roca, 13, 27, 29, *29*
Cabral, Pedro Álvares, 55, 56
Cacilhas drydocks, 80
Caetano, Marcello, 63
Cale. *See* Oporto.

de Camões, Luís, 15, 110, 124, 133, *133*
Camões Center, 110
Camões Day, 124
Camões Institute, 110
Cão, Diogo, 11
Cape Cross, 11
Cape Verde Islands, 46, 50, 52–53
Capelinhos volcano, 22
caravels (ships), 10, *10*, 51, *51*
Carlos I (king), 60
carob trees, 36
Cascais, 107–108
Castelo de São Jorge, 71
Catholicism, 43, 46, 54, 57, 62, *100*, 101–103, *101*, 105
Celtic migrants, 41
Christianity. *See* Catholicism.
Church of Sao Ildefonso, *100*
cities
  Angra do Heroísmo, 22
  Cascais, 107–108
  Coimbra, 25
  Estoril, 107–108
  Fátima, 104, 107
  Funchal, 23
  Ilhavo, 89
  life in, 124–125
  Lisbon, 23, *23*, 124–125
  Oporto, *19*, *25*, 68, *125*
  Sintra, 25, 109
  Viana Do Castelo, 79
climate, 16, 21, 27, *27*, 32
coastline, *14*, 15, 16, *20*, 36
cockerel (national symbol), 37, *37*
Coimbra, 25, 96, *97*, 98, *98*
colonization, 46–47, *48*, 52, 60, 62–63, 65
  Africa, 59, 63–64, *64*, 65
  map, *48*
Commission for Equality and Women's Rights, 67
Conferences at Berlin, 59–60, *59*
constitution, 58, 67, 72
Constitutional Tribunal, 70
copper mining, 91
cork, 19, 33, *33*, 34, *34*, 84, 85–87, *85*
Costa Verde, 36
Council of Ministers, 69
Council of State, 69, 70
Courts of Second Instance, 70
Crusades, 49
currency (escudo), 86, *86*, 87

D

Dias, Bartolomeu, 11, 51, 133
Dias, Dinís, 52
Douro River, 19, *19*, 24, 26, 43

E

earthquakes, 28, 109
economy
  agriculture, 32, 37, 41, 52–53, 62, *74*, 77, 82–84, *82*, 122
  bankruptcy, 60
  boat building industry, 80–81
  employment, 67, 87–88, 90, 91, 95
  escudo (currency), 86, *86*, 87
  fishing industry, 75–79, *75*, *76*, *78*, 83
  manufacturing, 25, 77, 89–91, *90*
  mining, 77, 91
  timber industry, 84
  tourism, 25, 27, 37, 87, 109, 127
  winemaking, 26, *26*, 36, 84–85, 88, *88*
education, 43, 56, 62, 93–94, 96–99, 122
emigration, 64
employment, 67, 87–88, 90, 91, 95
escudo (currency), 86, *86*, 87
Estoril, 107–108
Estremadura region, 17
eucalyptus trees, 32–33, 84
European Union (EU), 13, 38, 67, 75, 120–121

Eusebio (soccer player), 115, *115*, 133
Evora, 97–98
executive branch of government, 69, 70
exploration, *8*, 9–11, 13, 45–48, *47*, 56–57, 114, *114*
  astrolabe, 9–10, *9*, 46, *46*
  caravels, 10, *10*, 51, *51*
  map, *48*
  religion and, 52
  stone markers, 10–11, *10*
Expo '98, 71, 113, *113*

F

Fado Museum, 112
fado music, 99, 110–113
Fátima, 104, 107
"Ferryman" game, 114
Festival of São João, 122
Festival of Senhor Santo Cristo, 37
Festival of Sintra, 122
First Republic, 61, 102
fishing industry, 75–79, *75*, *76*, *78*, 83
foods, 76, 123
forests, 32–33, *32*
Fort Jesus, *11*
Forum Algarve, 127
Funchal, 23

G

da Gama, Vasco, 51, 53, 54, *54*, 133
games, 114
geography, 15
  borders, 15, 16, 26
  coastline, *14*, 15, 16, *20*, 36
  size, 15
geopolitical map, *12*
golden eagle, 38, *38*
Gomes, Fernão, 53
government, 44–45, 49
  Armed Forces movement, 64
  Assembly of the Republic, 70
  constitution, 58, 67, 72
  Constitutional Tribunal, 70
  Council of Ministers, 69
  Council of State, 69, 70
  Courts of Second Instance, 70
  districts, 70, 73
  employees of, 90
  executive branch, 69, 70
  First Republic, 61, 102
  judiciary branch, 69, 70
  legislative branch, 69, *69*, 70, 73
  religion and, 102
  Second Republic, 66–67
  Supreme Court, 70
Guadiana River, 26
Gulbenkian, Calouste, 112
Gulbenkian Museum, 112
Gulf of Cadiz, 26

H

Henriques, Alfonso, *44*, 45, 72
Henry of Burgundy, 44–45
Henry the Navigator, 8, 9, 49, 50, *50*, 103, 133
Hess, Walter Rudolph, 117
historical maps. *See also* maps.
  Exploration and Colonization, *48*
  Reconquest by Christians from the Moors, *45*
  Roman Iberia, *42*
housing, *18*, *30*, 31, 95, 124, *125*

I

Iberian lynx, 38
Iberian peninsula, 15
Iberian Union, 58
Ilhavo, 89
Inquisition, 57–58, *57*
Iron Age, 41
Islamic religion, 43–44, 109

J

Jeronimos Monastery, 103, *103*
Jiang Zemin, 73, *73*
João I (king), 49
João II (king), 49
João III (king), 57
João IV (king), 58
judiciary branch of government, 69, 70

L

language, 13, 43, 56, 96, 99, *99*
legislative branch of government, 69, *69*, 70, 73
Lisbon, 71
  Botanical Garden, 34, *106*
  earthquake in, 28
  Expo '98, 71, 113, *113*
  life in, 124–125
  map of, *71*
  as Olisipo, 42
  parliament building, 69
  Port of Lisbon, 79–80, *79*
  Rossio, 107
  Tagus River and, 23, *23*
  University of Lisbon, 96
  Zoological Garden, *31*
literacy rate, 93–94
literature, 107, 110, 117, *117*
loquat trees, 36
Lusitanian culture, 42
Lusitano horses, 38–39, *39*

M

Macao colony, 13, 48–49, 73
Machel, Samora, 65
Madeira Islands, 15, 21, 22–23, *30*, 46, 50, 52, 70, 73, 84–85
da Maia, Manuel, 28
Manuel I (king), 56–57, 133
Manuel II (king), 60
Manueline architecture, 103, *103*
manufacturing, 77, 90–91
  Coimbra, 25
  dinnerware, 89–90, *90*
maps. *See also* historical maps.
  geopolitical, *12*
  Lisbon, *71*
  natural resources, *84*
  population density, *96*
  provinces, *17*
  regions, *17*
  "rose-colored map," 60
  topographical, *16*
marine life, 75–79, *75*, *76*, 123
Marquês de Pombal, 28, *28*, 97
Mediterranean Sea, 29
mesticos (mixed-race people), 53
metric system, 86
military, 64–65
Minho region, 17, 36
mining, 77, 91
Misia (singer), 111–113, *111*
Moniz, Antõnio Caetano de Abreu Freire Egas, 117
Monument to the Discoverers, 114, *114*
Moorish culture, 21, 25, 43, 44, 58, 109
Mota, Rosa, 117, *117*
Museum of Sacred Art, 25
museums, 107
music, 107
  fado music, 99, 110–113
  Misia (singer), 111–113, *111*

N

national flag, 72, *72*
national holidays, 102
National Museum of Ancient Art, 113
National Palace, 109, *109*, 122
National Radio Broadcasting network, 111
natural resources map, 84
Neves Corvo copper mine, 91
Nobel Prize, 117, *117*

O

Olisipo. *See* Lisbon.
olive trees, 83, *83*
Op-Sail millennium event, 82
Oporto, *19*, 25, *25*, 43, 68, 97, *125*
Os Lusiadas (Luis de Camões), 110, 124
Our Lady of Fátima, 122

P

Park of the Nations, 71, 113
people, *92*, *93*, *118*, *119*
  Celtic migrants, 41
  education, 43, 56, 62, 93–94, 96–99, 122
  emigration, 64
  employment, 67, 87–88, 90, 91, 95
  ethnicity of, 93
  literacy rate, 93–94
  Lusitanian culture, 42
  mesticos (mixed-race), 53
  migrants, 95–96
  national personality, 119
  Phoenician migrants, 41
  population, 25, 93, 96
  refugees, 66, 94–95
Phelps, Elizabeth, 85
Philip II, king of Spain, 58
Phoenician migrants, 41
Pico Alto mountain, 18
Pico volcano, 22
plant life, *30*, *31*, 32–36, *36*
  almond trees, 35, *35*
  bougainvillea, 31, *31*
  carob trees, 36
  cork trees, 19, 33, *33*, 34, *34*, 84, 85–87, *85*
  eucalyptus trees, 32–33, 84
  forests, 32–33, *32*
  loquat trees, 36
Policarpo, Dom José, 105
population, 93
  Coimbra, 25
  density map, 96
  Funchal, 25
  Oporto, 25
  Sintra, 25
porcelain dinnerware, 89, *89*
Port of Lisbon, 79–80
Portuguese National Day, 124
Portuguese Navigators and Discoverers Monument, 71
Portuguese water dog, 39, *39*
provinces map, *17*

R

radio broadcasts, 111
refugees, 66, 94–95
regions map, *17*
religion
  beatification ritual, 104
  Catholicism, 43, 46, 54, 57, 62, *100*, 101–103, *101*, 105
  Church of Sao Ildefonso, *100*
  Cockerel of Suffering, 37
  Crusades, 49
  exploration and, 52
  festivals, 121–122
  government and, 102
  Inquisition, 57–58, *57*
  Islamic, 43–44, 109
  Jeronimos Monastery, 103, *103*
“Republicans,” 60, 61
Revolution of the Carnations, 64–65, *65*, 127
Rio de Janeiro (Brazil), 58
Rio Tejo. *See* Tagus River.
rivers
  Douro River, 19, *19*, 24, 26, 43
  Guadiana River, 26
  Tagus River, 16, 19, 23, *23*, 24, 41, 71

roadways, 42, 124
Rocha da Gale Reservoir, 16
Rodrigues, Amália, *111*
Roman occupation, *40*, 42–43, *42*
Rose Festival, *122*
"rose-colored map," 60

S

Sagres (ship), 82
Salazar, António de Oliveira, 61–63, *62*, 120
Salazar Bridge. *See* Twenty-Fifth of April Bridge.
Sampaio, Jorge, 73, *73*
dos Santos, Eugenio, 28
São Bento train station, 110
São Francisco Cellars Wine Museum, 25
Saraiva, Dom José, 105
Saramago, José, 110, 117, *117*
Sebastian (king), 58
Second Republic, 66–67
Senhor Santo Cristo Festival, 121, *121*
Serra da Estrela mountains, 16, 17–18, 19
Serra do Larouco mountains, 17, *18*
Serra do Monchique mountains, 21
shopping malls, 126–127, *126*
Silva, Anibal Cavaco, 67, 133
Sintra, 25, 109
Sintra Mountains, 25
slave trade, 11, 13, 47, 50, *50*, 53, 59
Soares, Mário, 67, 72, *72*
soccer, 107, 115, *115*
Social Democrats, 67
Spal dinnerware, 90, *90*
spice trade, 49
sports
- bullfighting, 116, *116*
- running, 117, *117*
- soccer, 107, 115, *115*

Stone Age, 41
Supreme Court, 70

T

Tagus River, 16, 19, 23, *23*, 24, 41, 71
Technical University of Lisbon, 96
Terceira Island, 22
timber industry, 84
Timor Island, 54–55
topographical map, *16*
tourism, 25, 27, 37, 87, 109, 127
Tower of Belém, 48
traineiras (trawlers), 76
Trás-os-Monte region, 17, 27
tungsten mining, 91
25th of April Bridge, 24, *24*

U

University of Coimbra, 96, *97*, 98, *98*
University of Evora, 97–98
University of Lisbon, 96
University of Oporto, 97

V

varinas (fishwives), 78, *78*
Viana Do Castelo, 79
Vila Franco do Lima, *122*
Vista Alegre dinnerware, 89
volcanoes, 16, 21, 22

W

wildlife. *See* animal life; marine life; plant life.
winemaking, 26, *26*, 36, 84–85, 88, *88*
World War II, 63

Z

Zoological Gardens, *31*

Meet the Authors

Ettagale Blauer and Jason Lauré have traveled to Portugal many times, sometimes together and sometimes with other people. "From the time of our first trips, in 1969 and 1970, to our most recent trip, in 2000, we have seen the changes in Portuguese society. The look of the cities and the countryside has not changed that much. The wonderful architecture, the stone sidewalks, the monuments and museums as well as the beaches and historical sites have scarcely changed at all. But the people on the street look very different today than they did thirty years ago. The young people, especially, are as up to date in their appearance as young people in other parts of Europe or in the United States. The increase in the use of English is one of the biggest changes. On our first trips, we struggled with language. We found few people who spoke English. Now, almost anyone we approach on the street or in a park or a shop speaks excellent English."

When Jason stood on the cliffs at Cabo da Roca, the westernmost point in Europe, he had a sense of the vastness of the

ocean faced by the Portuguese explorers. When Ettagale stood by the tile mural depicting Lisbon before the earthquake of 1755, she was struck by both the artistry of the tiles and the busy city they showed.

"The changes in the economy of Portugal were evident everywhere we went. Portuguese families had more money to spend and filled the restaurants, both in central Lisbon as well as in the residential suburbs.

"The essential character of the Portuguese people seems very much the same. People are reserved and polite, but the people we met and spoke with on our last trips were also more open in expressing their opinions. They wanted to talk about political issues that affected their lives and they were well informed about events taking place around the world.

The fishermen on the shore at Estoril, on the other hand, seemed to be exactly the same as the fishermen we saw thirty years ago. They mended their nets and tended their boats in the same, age-old ways. Portugal seems to have the best of both worlds right now, the old and the new."

Photo Credits

Photographs ©2002:

A Perfect Exposure: 7 bottom, 92 (Franck Iren/Author's Images), 103, 7 top, 24, 81, 88, 109 (Christine Pinheira/Author's Images), 33, 75 (Tony Steinhardt/Author's Images)

AKG London: 8, 9, 10 top, 46, 54, 55, 57, 62

AP/Wide World Photos/Luisa Ferreira: 66, 113

Corbis Images: 73, 94, 111 bottom, 111 top, 117 bottom (AFP), 31 right, 69, 82, 83, 98 (Tony Arruza), 65 (Bettman), 85 top (Jonathan Blair), 11 (Jan Butchofsky-Houser), 68 (Stephanie Colasanti), 32 (Ecoscene), 39 bottom (Kit Houghton Photography), 31 left (Wolfgang Kaehler), 80 (Stephanie Maze), 34, 85 bottom (Charles O'Rear), 115 top, 115 bottom (Reuters NewMedia Inc.), 117 top (Eye Ubiquitous), 44, 132 top (Nik Wheeler), 50 bottom

Dave G. Houser/HouserStock, Inc./ Jan Butchofsky: 110 top

Ettagale Blauer: 90

H. Armstrong Roberts, Inc.: 121 (George Hunter), 40 (W.J. Scott), 71 bottom (H. Sutton), 14, 29, 131 bottom (M. Thonig), 114 (A. Tovy)

Hulton Archive/Getty Images: 42 bottom, 64, 72 bottom

International Stock Photo: 25, 130 left (Loek Polders), 74, 125 (Stockman), back cover, cover, 6, 19, 26, 37, 118 (Paul Thompson), 106 (Chris Warren), 18 top (Hilary Wilkes-Ribeira), 30 (Hilary Wilks)

Jason Lauré: 10 bottom, 20, 23, 51, 86 left, 101, 112

MapQuest.com, Inc.: 72 top, 131 top

Mary Evans Picture Library: 50 top (Thomas Gillmor), 28 left, 59, 104, 110 bottom, 133 bottom

Nik Wheeler: 2, 76, 89, 108 top

Peter Arnold Inc.: 119, 133 top (Jeff Greenberg), 36 (Helga Lade)

Photo Researchers, NY: 35 (Richard L. Carlton), 38 (Jeff Lepore), 39 top (Bonnie Sue)

Superstock, Inc.: 22, 78 bottom, 97, 122

The Art Archive /Picture Desk: 28 right (Dagli Orti/Museo Nacional de Soares dos Reis Porto Portugal), 47 (Dagli Orti/Museu Historico Nacional Rio de Janeiro Brazil)

The Image Works: 86 right, 132 bottom (Markus Heimbach), 93 (Larry Mangino)

Visuals Unlimited/Jeff Greenberg: 99

Woodfin Camp & Associates: 18 bottom (Geoffrey Clifford), 78 top, 79, 100, 108 bottom, 126 (Robert Frerck), 116 (Jaques Lowe)

Maps by Joe LeMonnier